ROUTEMASTER
Jubilee

GEOFF RIXON

Ian Allan
PUBLISHING

Contents

Front cover: Prototype Routemaster RM2 stands at the Wandsworth terminus of route 91 shortly after entering Central Area service in the autumn of 1957. *Harry Luff*

Back cover (top): Freshly outshopped in its original London Transport Country Area green, Stagecoach in London RML2456 arrives at Victoria on route 8 on 30 March 2004. This vehicle was expected to pass into preservation following displacement from route 8 in June 2004. *Geoff Rixon*

Back cover (middle): As part of FirstGroup's contribution to celebrating 50 years of the Routemaster, First London RM1650 has been painted in its 1977 Silver Jubilee livery as SRM3. The bus is seen in St Mark's Road, Ladbroke Grove, soon after entering service on route 7 in April 2004. *Vernon Murphy*

Back cover (bottom): Withdrawn from service with Stagecoach in London when Upton Park garage's route 15 was converted to low-floor operation in August 2003, RML2565 passed to dealer Ensign of Purfleet, which duly transferred the vehicle to its Warwickshire-based Stratford Blue operating subsidiary. Freshly painted in traditional Stratford Blue livery of delphinium blue and ivory with silver roof, the bus was photographed at Wisley while attending the Cobham Bus Museum open day on 4 April 2004. *Geoff Rixon*

Title page: A view of the huge Stockwell garage (SW), with its roof span of 194ft by 378ft, which opened in April 1952. This photograph, taken in 1969, depicts a line of Routemasters all displaying blinds for route 88, but RMs also worked from this garage on routes 2 and 2A. Noticeable are various detail differences, with one bus displaying the raised bonnet badge as well as the later AEC-style triangle. *Bruce Jenkins*

Right: A slow trickle of the first production RMs started to be licensed for service by May and June 1959. New RM30 lays over at Crystal Palace while working from Cricklewood garage, which had five for trials on route 2. *Harry Luff*

First published 2004

ISBN 0 7110 2999 7

Published by Ian Allan Publishing

an imprint of Ian Allan Publishing Ltd, Hersham, Surrey KT12 4RG.

Printed by Ian Allan Printing Ltd, Hersham, Surrey KT12 4RG.

Code: 0409/C

Introduction

THERE are various ways of reviewing the remarkable 50-year life of the Routemaster (RM) bus. Previous books on the subject have mainly been structured according to vehicle types; *Routemaster Jubilee* adopts a different approach by looking at developments over the decades in which the vehicle has operated in public service, from the 1950s through to the present day (2004). Consequently, it is possible to present the photographs in approximate date order, from RM1's first appearance in 1954 to the last survivors still earning their keep in 2004.

The red Routemaster has become a London icon, like the Beefeaters and the Guardsmen, and has many unique claims to fame. For example, the Routemaster

- has lasted longer than any other bus in Britain, in terms of fleet operation
- is the only bus type to have become a household name
- is the last bus of traditional design (half-cab, open rear platform, front-engined) to remain in service in significant numbers
- is the only London bus type to have carried so many different liveries
- is the last bus type to operate in London which was specifically designed to meet London's demanding operational requirements.

The Golden Jubilee of the Routemaster is being marked in 2004 because it is 50 years since the first prototype was first unveiled to the public at the Commercial Motor Show. However, the type has been in service in London for 'only' 48 years, and it is now uncertain whether the Routemaster will still be gracing the streets of the capital in 2006. It was only a few years ago that Transport for London officials were scouring the country (including attending bus rallies!) to augment the reduced RM fleet (which had been decimated in the 1980s) in preparation for the planned expansion of bus services. Now that policy has been reversed, and Routemasters are being replaced in London with incredible haste, with all existing routes likely to receive new buses by 2005. Several factors seem to have influenced this change of heart, namely:

- the reduction in traffic arising from the congestion charge, making one-person operation more practicable
- off-bus ticketing, rendering conductors unnecessary
- the age of the vehicles, giving rise to mechanical problems
- insufficient passenger capacity of RMs
- the developing blame / litigation culture ('not *my* fault I fell off the platform', etc)

Admittedly we knew that Routemasters wouldn't last forever, but the speed of their final demise is surprising to many. The only ray of hope in London seems to be the possibility that a Routemaster-operated heritage service, covering London's main tourist attractions will be introduced; only time will tell. Nevertheless, it is conceivable that we will have to go outside London (*e.g.* to Edinburgh, which has a thriving tour fleet) or even abroad to see Routemasters operating in public service in the latter part of the current decade.

In putting together this tribute to the famous Routemaster bus, I should like to thank the large number of photographers featured in this book for letting me use their colour and black and white material. Thanks go also to Lizzy Tyler, for 'word-processing' this book, and to Kevin McCormack, for his support and assistance.

Geoff Rixon
East Molesey, Surrey
July 2004

On 1 August 1999 the Routemaster Operators & Owners Association held a rally at Lingfield in Surrey to celebrate the 45th anniversary of the Routemaster. Seen here is a selection of 15 preserved examples of the 40 Routemasters that attended. *Geoff Rixon*

1

The 1950s

THE Routemaster was conceived against the background of a need for a more modern bus than the RT type to meet London's longer-term requirements. The RT was basically a prewar design and did not reflect permitted increases in dimensions introduced in 1950 or new design developments which had potential for reducing operating costs. Also, at around this time the future of the trolleybus network was being questioned, and, if motor buses were to replace trolleybuses, it was preferable to use vehicles larger than RTs, which had limited capacity compared with trolleybuses. This increased the justification for a larger, modern bus. By 1954 a firm decision to replace most of the trolleybus network with buses had been taken by London Transport (LT), and this coincided with the construction of the prototype Routemaster.

The first four prototypes

RM1 was built at LT's Chiswick Works as a joint venture with AEC and Park Royal Vehicles and was unveiled to the public at the Commercial Motor Show at Earl's Court on 24 September 1954. The bus had many innovations, principally that it was of chassisless construction and built entirely from aluminium (apart from a fibreglass bonnet and rear upstairs window-frame), thereby reducing overall weight despite its increased passenger capacity. The Routemaster's main drawback, however, was that it was expensive to build and therefore beyond the means of most operators. During 1955 RM1 underwent extensive testing and considerable modification in preparation for its entry into public service on 8 February 1956.

The construction of RM2 followed on quickly from RM1, and the vehicle was completed by March 1955. Mechanically, RM2 was quite different from RM1, particularly with regard to steering and transmission. It was also fitted initially with a smaller engine to test fuel consumption, but during its trial period this was replaced by an engine of similar capacity to that fitted to RM1. The main external difference between the first two prototypes was that RM2 was painted in Country Area Lincoln green, and it was in this livery that it entered public service, on 20 May 1957.

For the third and fourth prototypes LT used suppliers other than AEC and Park Royal. Both vehicles were built with Leyland engines and running units, hence the letter 'L' in their RML and CRL designations; other Leyland-engined RMs were to follow later. However, these two Routemasters would be the only ones bodied by Weymann (RML3) or Eastern Coach Works (CRL4). RML3 was painted red and entered public service on 22 January 1958 following six months of trials. CRL4 was the most successful of the prototypes in terms of its long operational life and was visually the most impressive. It was designed as a Green Line coach (CRL standing for Coach Routemaster Leyland), complete with electronically operated platform doors, and the two-tone livery highlighting the raised window mouldings greatly enhanced its appearance. It entered public service on 9 October 1957.

The standard production RMs

In August 1956 LT received authorisation from the British Transport Commission to buy 1,520 Routemasters — virtually the number needed to replace the entire trolleybus fleet apart from the postwar 'Q1s'. Delivery was intended to commence late in 1958, in time for the start of the trolleybus-replacement programme in early 1959. However, only one Routemaster (RM8) was completed in 1958, and this was displayed at the Commercial Motor Show. However, unlike RM1 at the 1954 Motor Show, it made little impact because, in the intervening four years, bus technology had developed considerably. The rear-engined, front-entrance Leyland Atlantean had appeared at the 1956 Motor Show, and by 1958 the Routemaster, despite its advanced mechanics, was already looking old-fashioned.

The production RMs were closer in general appearance to RML3 than to the other prototypes. The first production RMs actually to belong to LT were RMs 6, 9 and 11, delivered in May 1959. (RM8, incidentally, was used as an experimental vehicle for much of its life, being subject to various modifications over the years and not entering normal service with LT until 1976.) A delivery flow then ensued, but too late for RMs to be used for the first stages of trolleybus replacement. Although the trolleys were old, they were reliable, whereas the RMs, like any new design, suffered teething problems and needed a further period of testing out of the limelight (alongside RTs) before being heralded as London's newest bus to replace the trolleybus. Surplus RTs, some of which had seen little previous use, were used for Stages 1-3 of trolleybus replacement.

Production RMs eventually entered service on 6 June 1959, when RMs 5, 7 and 24 began working route 8 from Willesden garage. But the RM finally came of age on 11 November 1959, when the class took over Poplar depot's three trolleybus routes.

RM1

RM1 was built at London Transport's Chiswick Works in 1954 and was first displayed at the 1954 Commercial Motor Show at Earls Court.
Its service life began on 8 February 1956 working out of Cricklewood garage on route 2. However, its operation was intermittent, and it returned from time to time to Chiswick Works for modifications to be carried out. In December 1959 it was overhauled at Aldenham Works and relicensed, but its short passenger life was over, and it became a fully fledged member of the training fleet, being used mostly by Upton Park garage. In 1964 a further trip to Aldenham Works preceded its reappearance with front end converted to match that of the standard production model. In 1972 RM1 was withdrawn and sold to the Lockheed Hydraulic Brake Co, which used it for PSV suspension trials, but in 1981 it was reacquired by London Transport and stored at Chiswick Works until refurbished by Aldenham Works apprentices in 1982.
Today it resides in London's Transport Museum at Covent Garden but has not had its original front end re-fitted.

The photograph above depicts RM1's second public appearance, still in 'as built' condition.
The occasion was the Aluminium Centenary Exhibition on London's South Bank in June 1955. Both before and after the exhibition RM1, accompanied by RM2, was undergoing extensive trials at various external locations.
Bruce Jenkins

Another view of RM1 at the Aluminium Industries exhibition held on the South Bank between 1 and 10 June 1955.
Bruce Jenkins

RM1 was first licensed for public service on 11 January 1956, and its very first service outing came on 8 February 1956 working from Cricklewood garage on route 2. It is seen here in the winter gloom at Golders Green bus station on its fourth day of service, Saturday 11 February. By now it had been fitted with new destination displays and a grille (below the front 'ultimate' blind box) for the heating and ventilation system. *Bruce Jenkins*

This offside view of RM1, surrounded by RTLs at Golders Green bus station on route 2 on 16 February 1956, shows the vehicle covered in winter road grime, due to the snowy conditions. *Bruce Jenkins*

This very rare early colour shot of RM1, working on route 2 in Vauxhall Bridge Road, was taken during its first few months of service, in May 1956. The vehicle was allocated to Cricklewood garage, where it had entered service in February 1956. By August the bus had returned to Chiswick Works for major alterations which saw its unique front panel replaced by the style fitted to the other three prototypes. *Bruce Jenkins*

In August 1956 RM1, having completed six months' service, returned to Chiswick Works for modifications to improve the airflow for cooling the radiator and brakes. It emerged in November to make a public appearance in the Lord Mayor's Show in the City of London, sporting a new-style grille with vertical bars and with its large LT bullseye badge replaced by a much smaller version. This view shows the bus in the parade line-up before the start of the procession. *Bruce Jenkins*

In 1957 RM1 was used on other routes operated by Cricklewood garage, in particular routes 1, 60 and 260. The bus is seen here on route 260 on Colindale station forecourt, rubbing shoulders with an RTW on route 60. Note that the vertical bars on the front grille, which it received in late 1956, have gone, replaced by a more conventional mesh grille. *Kevin Lane*

A winter picture of RM1 on the route 2 stand at Crystal Palace, taken in 1958 and showing the revised style of grille. By this time the bus had completed almost two years of service and was looking slightly careworn, with various panels repainted. But why it is posed alongside a prewar Lytham St Anne's Leyland is a mystery. *Harry Luff*

RM2 was taken into London Transport stock in March 1955 and over the next few months underwent various tests with RM1, for fuel consumption, strain gauge and endurance, at Northolt Airport, Nuneaton and Chobham. When the bus was ready for service the only visual difference externally from RM1 was its Country Area green livery. Allocated to Reigate garage, it entered service on 20 May 1957, working on route 406. In this view, recorded during its first few days of service, RM2 prepares to start its journey from Redhill to Kingston. *Bruce Jenkins*

RM2

Like RM1, the second prototype Routemaster was a joint venture by London Transport and AEC/Park Royal Vehicles. Painted in Country Area green with a cream relief band, RM2 entered service on 20 May 1957, running alongside RTs on routes 406 and 406A from Reigate garage. Following gearbox problems RM2 returned to Chiswick on 8 August 1957. This marked the end of its Country Area life for, on return to service, it was repainted in Central Area red and allocated to Turnham Green, which garage was close to Chiswick Works and thus convenient should any problems occur. After driver training, the bus started stage-carriage work on route 91, and it remained in service intermittently,

when it was not receiving attention at Chiswick Works. By 1 November 1959, having reached the end of its service life, RM2 was demoted to a training vehicle, lasting as such until 1972. Like RM1, it had its front end replaced by the standard design in 1964. From 1972 it was used at Chiswick for experimental purposes, which included trying out the 1977 Silver Jubilee and 1979 Shillibeer liveries, until closure of the works in 1986. It is now part of London's Transport Museum collection and at the time of writing (July 2004) was being restored to its original green livery. Plans are in hand to re-fit the original-style front.

This very rare picture of RM2 was taken during its short spell working in the Country Area on route 406 in June 1957 and may well be the only colour record of RM2 in green livery. The vehicle is travelling along the Epsom Road, Ewell on the A24, just before turning off for Ewell Village on its way to Kingston. *John Webb*

Another rare picture, showing RM2 soon after starting service on route 91 in the Central Area. The bus is standing at the route's Carnwath Road, Wandsworth, terminus in early autumn 1957.
Harry Luff

On 8 August 1957 RM2's short Country Area life ended and the bus returned to Chiswick Works. The out-of-town route 406 had not proved to be an ideal testing-ground for a prototype, and, in any case, transmission problems were occurring which required rectification. At the end of August 1957 RM2 reappeared sporting Central Area red livery and was allocated to Turnham Green garage for use on route 91. The bus is seen here having a break from everyday service, attending a bus rally at the AEC works at Southall in 1958.
Phil Tatt

The first Leyland-engined prototype, numbered RML3, was built at the Weymann factory in Addlestone, where this picture was taken in 1957 while the bus was still in grey primer. Although structurally complete and thus able to undertake testing, it was little more than a shell at this stage, as the interior had yet to be fitted out. *Geoff Rixon*

RML3

Fitted with Leyland (rather than AEC) running units, RML3 was taken into LT stock from Weymann's on 1 July 1957. However, the vehicle was to carry out further evaluation trials at Leyland's works in Lancashire and would not enter service until 22 January 1958, when it started work from Willesden garage on routes 8 and 8B. Unfortunately, while working in the Edgware Road on route 8 in January 1959, this prototype was involved in an accident in which it sustained extensive front-end damage; duly repaired, it returned to service on 1 March. Just eight months later, however, its life as a public service vehicle was over, as on 1 November 1959 it was transferred (with RMs 1 and 2) as a permanent driver-training bus, based at Upton Park garage. Subsequently renumbered RM3, to avoid confusion with the 30ft Routemasters, it also had its front end rebuilt to conform with later buses. Withdrawn by LT in 1972, it is now preserved by the London Bus Preservation Trust at Cobham Bus Museum, which restored its original frontal design to coincide with the RM50 celebrations in 2004.

RML3 was taken into LT stock from Weymann's on 1 July 1957. However, the vehicle was to carry out further evaluation trials at Leyland's works in Lancashire and would not enter service until 22 January 1958, when it started work from Willesden garage on routes 8 and 8B. This picture shows it on the stand for route 8 at the Willesden terminus in May 1958. *Bruce Jenkins*

Early colour material of the prototype Routemasters — like this picture of Leyland-engined RML3, taken after it had completed its first two months in service — is hard to come by. The bus is seen emerging from Park Lane into Marble Arch on Sundays-only route 8B from Willesden garage, where it would remain allocated for the rest of its (short) service life. Relegated to use as a driver trainer, it was renumbered RM3 in September 1961, when the letter 'L' came to signify a 30ft length rather than a Leyland engine. *Bruce Jenkins*

Left: The first prototype Routemaster Green Line coach, built by Eastern Coach Works at its factory in Lowestoft, Suffolk, was also fitted with a Leyland engine and was classified CRL (**C**oach **R**outemaster **L**eyland). Handed over to London Transport on 14 June 1957 (a few weeks ahead of RML3), CRL4 is seen here shortly after delivery. *Geoff Rixon collection*

Below: CRL4 started its service life on 9 October 1957 allocated to Romford (RE), from which garage it worked the busy East End Green Line route 721 (Romford–Aldgate). This view shows the vehicle at Aldgate bus station on 29 December 1957. It was transferred to Reigate just 10 days later, on 8 January 1958, by which time it had covered 7,000 miles in public service. *Colin Brown*

CRL4

The second Leyland Routemaster prototype was CRL4, with Eastern Coach Works bodywork fitted out to full Green Line specification complete with deep-cushioned seats, parcel racks and electrically operated platform doors. Entering service on 9 October 1957, it worked initially from Romford (RE) garage alongside RTs on route 721. Renumbered in August 1961 as RMC4, like the other three prototypes it had its original bonnet assembly rebuilt to standard pattern (incorporating the twin headlamps of the later RMCs) in 1964. On 1 January 1970 it passed to the newly formed London Country Bus Services and upon overhaul in 1976 gained NBC bus livery of leaf green with white waistband, having been demoted from regular Green Line use. Withdrawn from normal service in 1979, it remained with London Country, restored to Green Line livery as a 'special events' vehicle; surviving the division of the company in 1986, it passed to London Country (South West) — later London & Country — and was eventually sold into private preservation in 2000.

CRL4 was renumbered RMC4 in August 1961, when allocated to Stevenage for Green Line routes 716 (Hitchin–Chertsey) and 716A (Stevenage–Woking), on which it had operated since August 1960. This picture, taken in August 1962, shows the vehicle on route 716A, making its way through Stevenage on the long journey to Woking. *Bruce Jenkins*

Following spells at Stevenage and Hertford garages, RMC4 joined the new RMC fleet at Epping (to work Green Line routes 718, 720 and 720A) in February 1963, by which time it was the only one of the four Routemaster prototypes still in service. It is seen on 12 April about to leave Harlow for Aldgate on route 720. By April 1964 it had been delicensed for a long overdue overhaul and disappeared into Chiswick Works, where it lost its original style front end, returning to service at Harlow on 9 December looking like a standard RMC. *Gerald Mead*

Although RM8 was the first production RM to be built, RM6 was the first actually owned by LT, being delivered on 11 May 1959. RM6 was photographed soon after entering service in November 1959 from West Ham garage, being seen on route 272 under the trolleybus wires at Stratford Broadway in February 1960. *Bruce Jenkins*

Allocated to Willesden — the first garage to put production Routemasters into revenue-earning service — to work alongside RM5, RM7 was first licensed in June 1959 and is seen shortly afterwards at High Holborn on route 8. Withdrawn in August 1985 after a working life of 26 years, it is now preserved in Yorkshire. *Bruce Jenkins*

RM8 spent the first 18 years of its life as a Chiswick Works experimental vehicle and is seen in 1961 on trade plates. Built with a production-style RM front end, it was by now fitted with a modified version (not dissimilar to that on the prototypes), with large 'cage' vents for improved engine and brake cooling. *Geoff Rixon collection*

Right: RM95 started its service life at Turnham Green garage in October 1959 but did not remain there for long, moving to Poplar garage for trolleybus-replacement work the following month. The bus is photographed here on the stand at Clerkenwell Green on a Sunday working on route 5 early in 1960. It would be one of the early withdrawals from service, going to the breakers in August 1983.
Bruce Jenkins

The trolleybus wires from East London Circular trolleybus routes 689 and 690 are still in evidence in this view of RM197 operating new route 162 following completion of Stage 5 of the conversion programme. Entering service from West Ham garage, RM197 is seen on the stand at Stratford Broadway. This bus would end its service life in January 1990 at Palmers Green garage, being then sent to Barnsley for scrap.
Kevin Lane collection

First licensed in June 1959, RM18 was allocated new to Battersea garage (B), but was quickly transferred to Hackney (H), being seen in July 1959 at Holborn on route 22. It would remain at work in London, latterly from Brixton (BN) on South London Transport routes 137 and 159, until involved in an accident in 1996, being then withdrawn for scrap.
Gerald Mead

The Routemaster design was of chassisless construction with front and rear subframes, known as the 'A' and 'B' frames. Complete front-unit assemblies are seen here at the AEC works at Southall in September 1960. *Bruce Jenkins*

All production Routemaster bodies were built by Park Royal Vehicles, using aluminium alloy to reduce weight and improve fuel economy. RM540, seen taking shape in the main works body shop in September 1960, would be licensed and placed in service working from Hanwell garage in December. *Bruce Jenkins*

2

The 1960s

THE 1960s was the decade in which virtually all the Routemaster buses entered service, aside from the 176 which had taken to the streets of London by the end of 1959. In all, some 2,876 Routemasters would be built, encompassing several variations to the standard production RMs as well as two small batches which were not destined for London Transport.

July 1961 witnessed the arrival of something extraordinary: a London Transport Central Area bus which was not painted red (or wartime brown) — a concept that would be quite commonplace in the following decade. The pioneer was RM664, nicknamed the 'Silver Lady' because its aluminium body was left unpainted so that it could be compared, in terms of wear and maintenance, with those painted red. The experiment had worked for underground trains but failed to do so as far as RM664 was concerned for a variety of reasons, not least because it quickly became scruffy in appearance.

The next development was, in many ways, overdue — a lengthened Routemaster to take advantage of the extension of the permitted maximum for two-axle buses by 2ft 6in to 30ft, thereby increasing passenger capacity from 64 to 72 seats. The first RMLs (the 'L' now standing for 'lengthened') entered service on trolleybus-replacement route 104 (superseding trolleybus route 609) on 8 November 1961. There would eventually be 524 RMLs, including 100 for the Country Area.

Moving on to 1962, RMs completed the trolleybus conversion programme on 9 May and, from later in the year, started the mass replacement of the RT family. The same year also saw the production of a batch of 68 standard-length Green Line coach Routemasters, designated RMC, largely based on the prototype coach, CRL4. Apart from the fact these were the only standard-length Routemasters to be delivered in green livery, they also differed externally from their red bus counterparts by the fitting of twin headlights, a different blind display and rear platform doors. Internal differences included fluorescent lighting, luggage racks and more comfortable seats. The class was also fitted with improved suspension, and a high-speed differential. The first RMCs entered service on Green Line route 715 on 29 August 1962.

In October 1962 a Routemaster was once again the subject of attention at a Commercial Motor Show. The vehicle in question was RMF1254, the first forward-entrance Routemaster, designed so that it could quite easily be adapted for one-person operation. Using mainly standard components, it was the same length as the RMLs. After the show, RMF1254 entered service on 29 October, not in London but in Liverpool! Over the next 10 months it made two other visits to provincial operators in the hope of attracting orders for Routemasters, but to no avail. However, RMF1254 did achieve success when, in 1964, it was demonstrated with a luggage trailer in tow. For just over two years it worked between London and Heathrow Airport alongside the fleet of 1½-deck coaches belonging to British European Airways (BEA) so that the concept of double-deckers towing luggage trailers could be evaluated as a possible replacement for the existing coaches which were now becoming too small for BEA's needs. Meanwhile, in 1963, a surprise provincial order for Routemasters was placed by Northern General (the only operator outside London to buy new Routemasters), which took 50 forward-entrance 30ft buses similar to RMF1254, the first entering service on 1 May 1964.

Further Routemaster developments (in terms of vehicle types) followed in 1965. The last standard RMs for LT were delivered in May, after six years of production. The initial batch of 24 RMLs built in 1961 had proved very successful and formed the template for the future. However, the first longer vehicles to roll off the production line after the last standard RMs were 43 Green Line coaches, designated RCL (Routemaster Coach Lengthened), which, their greater length aside, closely resembled the RMCs. The RCLs were delivered in May and June and were luxurious compared to the Green Line RT buses they replaced on certain routes. These were followed by standard RML buses, mainly in Central Area red but also including 100 green Country Area examples.

In September 1966 there was a break in RML production, lasting for seven months, while 65 standard-length Routemasters were built for BEA. This reversion to the 27ft 6in length resulted from legislation which prevented longer vehicles (such as RMF1254, which had been given special dispensation) from towing trailers. Nevertheless, the experimental use of RMF1254 with luggage trailer attached had proved that the concept was viable and had secured this valuable contract. Delivery of the BEA Routemasters, which, like RMF1254, had forward entrances with doors, commenced at the end of October 1966. At the same time RMF1254 was withdrawn from BEA service and, because it closely matched Northern General's fleet of Routemasters, was fitted with a Leyland engine and sold to that operator in November 1966.

While these Routemaster developments were taking place, something much more radical was happening behind closed doors — a flat-fronted, rear-engined Routemaster was being constructed. The lead-in time for this project was considerable, and by the time the FRM (front-engined Routemaster) made its first public appearance in December 1966 (having missed the Commercial Motor Show), its fate was sealed. LT had shown that it could operate off-the-peg buses, having invested in some Leyland Atlanteans in 1965, and the cost of building a new generation of Routemasters was not an economic proposition.

There may also have been pressure from Leyland, which by now owned AEC, to buy its 'own' model rather than a niche-market bus which would be unlikely to appeal to other operators. FRM1 entered service in June 1967, but no more were built.

The start of 1968 saw the end of Routemaster production, with RML2760 being numerically the end of the line, although the last to be delivered were RML2754/6 on 8 February 1968. The Routemaster had become an obsolete design; indeed, double-deckers in general were considered to have a limited future, with high-capacity single-deckers being regarded as offering the brightest future for public road transport.

As the decade ended, one further major development was to occur to the London Routemaster, the effects of which would be seen in the 1970s. In August 1969 there appeared the first London bus to carry all-over advertising — RM1737. Even later in 1969 came the first colour change between red and green Routemasters (apart from RM2), when, for reasons that will be explained further in Chapter 3, RMLs 2321, 2441 and 2443 from the batch of 100 Country Area buses were repainted red and transferred to the Central Area.

The 1960s had witnessed the final development of the Routemaster in its various guises. However, public transport requirements were changing, economies (particularly with regard to manning levels) had to be made, and LT was increasingly coming under pressure from national and local government. The outlook for the Routemaster as it entered the 1970s was bleak.

RM664 was nicknamed the 'Silver Lady' because of its experimental unpainted alloy finish, (apart from fibreglass parts, such as the bonnet, which were painted silver). This was born of an idea to reduce running costs by reducing weight and had already been tried on Underground stock. Licensed from 13 July 1961 and allocated initially to Highgate for route 276 (and 127 on Sundays), the bus is seen leaving Brixton garage shortly after entering service. It was widely used, operating out of 10 other garages between December 1962 and August 1965, after which it was repainted red and allocated to New Cross, the experiment having been deemed a failure. *Harry Luff*

Another view of RM664 in its unpainted aluminium finish. This photograph of the 'Silver Lady' was taken in Whitehall on Sunday 14 October 1961. RM664's original body ended up on RM577, which, following withdrawal by LT, worked for Southend Transport and Reading Mainline and since 1999 has been in the hands of a preservationist. *Gerald Mead*

For just over six months in 1961 Sunday working of trolleybus route 609 produced the very unusual sight of Routemasters operating alongside trolleybuses. This arose from a need to provide overtime opportunities at Highgate garage, which had already lost its trolleybuses; Finchley depot, the normal operator of the 609, retained its fleet until 7 November 1961. RM581 entered service on the 609 at Highgate garage in February 1961. Following withdrawal in 1985 it would be sold to Stephen Austin Newspapers of Hertford and converted to open-top. *Gerald Mead*

Allocated to Shepherds Bush garage (S), RM338 is seen on route 268 in 1964, shortly after its first overhaul. The most noticeable difference since new is that the offside route-number box has been panelled over; the vehicle still retains its brake-cooling grilles, but eventually these too would be panelled over. *Colin Brown*

The RMLs

In 1961 the first 30ft-long Routemasters were delivered, the extra length being achieved by adding a short (2ft 4in) bay amidships, enabling the seating capacity to be increased from 64 to 72. An initial batch of 24 was constructed and numbered from 880 to 903 in the normal RM fleetnumber sequence. At first they were designated ERM (Extended Routemaster), but only the first four vehicles actually carried this, as the designation was changed to RML (the 'L' being reascribed to denote 'lengthened' rather than Leyland, as in the case of prototypes RML3 and CRL4). In November 1961 this first batch of RMLs started life allocated to Finchley (FY) garage to work trolleybus-replacement route 104. The main batch of RMLs was built between 1965 and 1968 and numbered RML2261-2760; of these 500 buses, 100 (RML2306-55 and 2411-60) were for the Country Area, while 100 of the Central Area vehicles (RML2561-2660) were noteworthy in being fitted with exterior illuminated advertising panels on the offside.

Of 97 RMLs which passed to London Country in 1970, most were re-purchased in the late 1970s by London Transport and returned to service as red buses, although a few were considered beyond redemption and sold for scrap after yielding spare parts. Otherwise the class remained largely intact until 2003 (thanks to major refurbishment in the 1990s), but withdrawals have gathered pace in 2004 as RMLs are replaced with Mercedes articulated vehicles and low-floor OPO double-deckers, and few are expected to survive in London into 2005.

Built in 1961, the 24 buses which constituted the first batch of RMLs all started life working from Finchley garage. RML892 stands at the Moorgate terminus of route 104 in August 1966. *Gerald Mead*

Godstone garage required 28 buses for Country Area routes 409, 410 and 411, upon which new green RMLs were due to start operating from 1 October 1965. The first, RML2306, arrived in September 1965, but with insufficient green examples being delivered, 17 newly built red RMLs were borrowed to help out. One of the red vehicles, RML2305, was caught travelling through leafy Coulsdon on route 409 in October 1965. *Gerald Mead*

Built for use in the Central Area, red RML2288 was delivered at around the time that the first green Country Area vehicles were entering service. However, due to slow delivery of the latter, it first entered service life on loan to the Country Area, being allocated to Godstone garage (GD) for routes 409, 410, 411 and 482. It is seen here picking up passengers on the 411 at the Red Cross, Reigate, in October 1965. *Roy Hobbs*

The Country Area's new green Routemasters were first licensed in October 1965 for use from Godstone garage. RML2313 is seen here laying over on route 410 at the Hardwick Road stand in Reigate during the first week of operation. *Roy Hobbs*

Early in 1966 some 40 new RMLs were delivered to West Ham, Walthamstow and Poplar garages for the 5-group routes and the 249A. West Ham was the main recipient, Poplar receiving nine for its minority share of the 5-group routes, including RML2410, seen at Shoreditch on 20 August 1966 on the Saturdays-only 5C. In 2003, by which time it was working from Arriva's Brixton garage, this bus had the misfortune to crash into a house (due to brake failure) and was consequently withdrawn from service. *Gerald Mead*

The trial installation of a Leyland engine in new RM632 in January 1961 resulted in an order for 406 similarly powered buses. RM870, built in September 1961, was the first of these and was allocated to Hanwell to work on route 207, which replaced trolleybus route 607.
It is pictured arriving at the Ealing Common stop when just a few months old, in March 1962. *Colin Brown*

Stonebridge Park garage (SE) received its first new Routemasters in January/February 1962 for replacement of trolleybus routes 660 and 666, which then became bus routes 260 and 266. It also required RMs for its share of route 18, which was extended to London Bridge, newly delivered RM1099 and RM1103 being seen at the Edgware terminus soon after the route was extended. *Colin Brown*

In January 1962 Middle Row garage (X) received an initial allocation of 14 new Routemasters for route 18, shared with Stonebridge Park. RM1012 is seen on the stand at Edgware in July 1963. *Gerald Mead*

Preserved 'Diddler' trolleybus No 1 returned to its old home of Fulwell depot (FW) in advance of the trolleybuses' last day, when it would work a special carrying the mayor and his entourage.
It is seen posing in the depot yard on 29 April 1962 with RM1078, which had started life in service from West Ham but had been transferred to Fulwell as a type trainer for the latter's forthcoming fleet. *Nick Lera*

London's last trolleybus routes were those in West London (operated from Fulwell and Isleworth depots), which survived until 8 May 1962. Replacement was effected by 82 new Routemasters delivered to Fulwell, Norbiton and Hounslow garages. Fulwell-operated routes 601, 602, 603, 604, 605 and 667 were replaced by bus routes 281, 282, 283, 285 and 267, while Isleworth's 657 was covered by extending Hounslow's 117. Fulwell's RM1100 approaches Teddington railway bridge on route 281 on 12 May 1962. *Geoff Rixon*

Norbiton garage (NB) received 20 of the new RMs to replace trolleybus routes 602, 603 and 604 on 8 May 1962. The 602 and 603 were replaced by new bus routes 282 and 283, while the 604 was covered by the existing 131. RM1210, the last of Norbiton's batch of new RMs, was photographed at the Tolworth terminus of the 283 with just a few days of service under its belt. *Geoff Rixon*

RM1074, allocated to Fulwell garage, prepares to leave Hammersmith for Hampton Court on route 267 in March 1963. First licensed in February 1962, this bus was allocated from new to Stonebridge Park but went on loan to Fulwell in April 1962 as a type trainer, before the latter garage received its own fleet of Routemasters to replace the trolleybuses in May 1962; RM1074 stayed on at Fulwell as part of its allocation. *Gerald Mead*

One of 40 new RMs allocated to Fulwell in May 1962 for trolleybus replacement, RM1118 crosses Teddington railway bridge bound for London (Heathrow) Airport on route 285. This was basically the old 605 trolleybus route extended from Teddington to replace part of two other routes — the 152 to Feltham station and the 90B thence to Harlington Corner. *Gerald Mead*

Starting in the early 1960s, Routemasters became ambassadors abroad, visiting 13 different countries on three continents, and between 1961 and 1975 no fewer than 52 RMs and RMLs carried the famous 'GB' plates. One of the first was RM546, which undertook three different tours; this picture was taken on 24 May 1962 at a trade fair in Stockholm, during its third and final tour. Following withdrawal from London service in December 1985 this bus worked for Clydeside Scottish, Western Scottish and Southend Transport and now resides in Germany, where it has been since 1996. *Les Folkard*

The finishing shops at AEC's Southall works in July 1962, with Green Line RMC coaches rubbing shoulders with the latest batch of red Central Area buses. RM1286 in the foreground would not enter service until December 1962 (from Tottenham garage), but RMC1460 would be one of the first its type into service, on route 715 in late August 1962. *Geoff Rixon*

Completed in 1962, RMF1254 was the first Routemaster to be built with a forward entrance.
As such it was non-standard to LT and ended up joining the 50 similar vehicles built subsequently
for Northern General. This picture was taken at Heathrow Airport during its stint with BEA
on the West London Air Terminal service, which was operated on BEA's behalf by LT. *Harry Luff*

RMF1254

The first Routemaster built with a forward entrance was handed over by Park Royal to LT in October 1962 and immediately undertook one month's trial operation in Liverpool, with the intention of attracting provincial orders. Upon its return it went into store at Aldenham, remaining there until March 1963, when it went on loan to East Kent at Canterbury. A month later the bus was back at Aldenham, where it remained out of the limelight for over a year. However, during this time it was used for testing purposes, to pilot a new style of headlight panel (without ventilator grilles) and a smaller air intake below the front blind box (allowing the central relief band to be continuous). These changes were subsequently adopted as standard for all Routemasters.

While RMF1254 was out of use the Ministry of Transport was considering permitting buses to pull trailers, and RMF1254 was duly fitted for this purpose to act as a guinea pig, in August 1964 joining the BEA fleet of $1^1/_2$-deck coaches. Aside from a fortnight serving as a demonstrator in Halifax, it spent the next two years with BEA, being withdrawn in October 1966 because by then new legislation had come into force restricting the length of buses permitted to tow trailers (which RMF1254 exceeded). The following month it was sold to Northern General, joining that company's fleet of 50 very similar buses, which it served for 14 years. After a long period of inactivity the bus was restored to LT condition in time for the RM50 celebrations in July 2004.

The RMCs

Following trials with prototype Leyland/ECW CRL4 (later RMC4), some 68 standard-length AEC/Park Royal Routemasters were ordered for Green Line work, these materialising in 1962 as RMC1453-1520. First entering service on 29 August 1962 on route 715, the type was allocated throughout the Country Area, and on 1 January 1970 all 68 passed to London Country Bus Services.

Replaced on Green Line services in 1972, the RMCs were demoted to bus work and started to receive the new LCBS bus livery of dark green with yellow waistband; later the same year, however, this colour scheme was itself superseded upon the introduction of NBC's corporate image, and most RMCs were ultimately repainted in leaf green with white waistband. However, by the mid-1970s the continuing spread of one-person operation was rendering the RMCs surplus even on bus work, and in 1977 London Transport began to reacquire them — a process completed by 1980. However, none re-entered passenger service at that time, most being used on driver-training work and many retaining green livery with LT roundels applied thereto.

In 1981 London Transport began to dispose of the RMCs, some of which passed directly into preservation. Despite this, a handful remained and, suitably overhauled, finally entered Central London service in March 1989 on route X15; as such they passed into Stagecoach ownership upon the privatisation of London Buses, and three remained in use, by now on route 15, until its conversion to low-floor operation in August 2003.

This cabside view shows one of the first production coaches, RMC1460, receiving final touches in the finishing shops at the AEC works in July 1962. It was first licensed in August 1962, when it entered service from Guildford garage on Green Line route 715. *Geoff Rixon*

The first of the new RMC coaches entered service on lengthy Green Line route 715, shared by Hertford and Guildford garages. Brand-new RMC1462 arrives at Hammersmith Butterwick bus station *en route* to Guildford in August 1962. Following its stint with London Country in the 1970s and subsequent return to LT in 1977, this vehicle was used as a driver-trainer until sold for preservation in the late 1980s. By 1992, however, it had joined the fleet of Nostalgiabus, working a few special journeys from Dorking to Horsham on route 93; in 1997 it was repainted in that company's attractive livery of red and cream for use on its short-lived Routemaster-worked route 306 (Epsom–Kingston) and in 1999 was one of a motley collection of vehicles to help out on LT route 60 (Streatham–Old Coulsdon), after the company operating that service ran into difficulties. *Colin Brown*

The second Green Line route converted from the single-deck RF type to the new RMC Routemaster coach was the 718 (Harlow–Windsor), in October 1962. The RMCs used thereon were allocated initially to Epping and Windsor garages; however, this was a short-lived move, as Epping garage was about to close in favour of a new garage at Fourth Avenue, Harlow, which opened on 22 May 1963, its initial allocation including 16 RMCs (including RMC4) — more than any other garage. This picture of RMC1486 was taken on 1 June 1963, shortly after its move to Harlow, which town it is about to leave, with a full complement of passengers, on its long journey to Windsor. *Gerald Mead*

Having entered service in January 1963, RMC1507 looked still to be in pristine condition when photographed passing Marble Arch on lengthy Green Line route 716 to Hitchin in August 1965. Following its spell with London Country in the 1970s this vehicle returned to LT ownership, ending its working life as a driver trainer at Stonebridge Park garage before passing into preservation in 1981. *Geoff Rixon*

Muswell Hill garage (MH) received a batch of 31 Routemasters in June/July 1963, mainly for route 43 but also used on Sundays on routes 102, 134A and 212. This picture shows RM1641 travelling through the quiet streets of Stroud Green on the 212 one Sunday in September 1965, its passengers apparently reluctant to go upstairs. Note that it carries both the LT roundel on the bonnet and the later triangular badge atop the radiator grille. *Gerald Mead*

In April/May 1964 Croydon garage (TC) was due to receive Routemasters for routes 68, 130A, 130B and 130C. However, at the same time Upton Park (U) garage needed a large number of new RMs for its east–west trunk route 15 (and the inter-worked 100), and its needs took priority, so Croydon received only six new vehicles (RM1900/1/3/4/6/7), the remainder of its requirement being met by vehicles transferred from Dalston and Hendon. RM1903 is seen on route 68 in Woburn Place, Bloomsbury, in August 1964. Croydon's turn would come late in 1967, when it took delivery of 36 new RMLs. *Gerald Mead*

With trolleybus replacement complete, new RMs started replacing the RT family on Central London routes, one of the first to receive RMs being the 36. Seen waiting to leave the West Kilburn stand, Leyland-engined RM1534 entered service from Peckham in March 1963. A subtle difference from earlier buses is apparent in the radiator grille, with the thick aluminium trim replaced with a smaller-gauge stainless-steel trim and a central vertical strip added. *Colin Brown*

The 2,056th Routemaster to come off the production line, standing outside the AEC works at Southall ready for delivery to Victoria garage in 1964. This vehicle was the last in a batch of 30 to go to Victoria for its share of route 137, operated jointly with Norwood. It was also one of the last to be built with the original, full-size heating/ventilation air-intake; from November 1964 Routemasters had the smaller intake, permitting the cream waistband to continue uninterrupted around the front. *Colin Brown*

The BEA batch aside, the last standard-length Routemaster to be built, in September 1965, was RM2217, which brought to 2,120 the total of production RMs. Around this time there was a minor livery change, the cream relief band being changed to grey. Soon after entering service, from Willesden garage, RM2217 battles with the traffic in Buckingham Palace Road while on route 46. *Bruce Jenkins*

With the success of the first batch of 24 RMLs, built in late 1961 and operating from Finchley garage on route 104, the decision was taken to build 43 30ft Routemaster coaches, classified RCL, with numbers (from 2218) following on from the last RM. All were delivered in June/July 1965, Grays garage receiving nine for route 723A, which started on 1 July. RCL2254 is seen during its first fortnight in service, at East Ham on 1 August 1965. This vehicle has been in preservation since withdrawal from LT service in 1984.
Gerald Mead

The RCLs

The only 30ft Routemaster coaches, the 43 RCLs were constructed during May and June 1965 and numbered RCL2218-60, powered by AEC AV690 11.3-litre engines. These were the heaviest Routemasters and were intended to replace the RT type on East London Green Line routes. The first batch started work on route 721 on 2 June 1965 from Romford garage, and two weeks later Romford's 722 was converted; by 1 July Grays garage had received an allocation for routes 723 and 723A, while a surprise was the allocation of five to Hertford, where they replaced RMCs to provide greater capacity on the 715.

With the formation on 1 January 1970 of London Country Bus Services the RCLs lost the large 'LONDON TRANSPORT' transfers situated between the decks, and by 1972 all the Green Line routes (except the 709, which retained three RCLs until May 1976) had been converted to OPO; the RCLs thus displaced were demoted to bus work, working from Crawley, Dorking, Grays and Reigate. By 1974 a repaint programme had seen many RCLs receive NBC leaf green.

London Transport's policy of purchasing Routemasters surplus to the needs of other operators eventually saw the return from LCBS ownership of most of the RCLs, some of which, relegated to the LT training fleet, received white 'bullseye' roundels on their NBC green livery. In January 1979 RCL2221 was converted into a mobile cinema and exhibition unit and donned the Shillibeer livery also carried

by 12 RMs to celebrate the 150th anniversary of George Shillibeer's first London omnibus service.

The most surprising development came in 1980, when LT decided to refurbish the RCL class for further PSV service, and 40 duly underwent a full overhaul at Aldenham Works. External modifications included the removal of the platform doors and the replacement of the twin headlamps with standard single units as fitted to RMs and RMLs; internal changes included the removal of the luggage racks, while the seating was reupholstered in DMS-style blue moquette. Re-entering service from August 1980, the type was allocated initially to Stamford Hill garage to operate route 149, but two months later a further batch was allocated to Edmonton garage, ostensibly for the same route but occasionally straying onto the 279.

By late 1984 all had been taken out of service and placed in store, but in 1986 11 of the survivors were overhauled at Aldenham, to work alongside standard Routemasters on the Original London Sightseeing Tour; this involved a repaint in red with gold LT fleetnames and numbers and the re-installation of platform doors (albeit of a different design). In 1990 10 of these were further modified to convertible-open-top format. The remainder of the class were sold off, some to small operators, others to restaurant owners etc, while yet others passed into preservation. Of the original total of 43, some 21 survive today in one form or another.

Grays garage received nine new RCL coaches for Green Line routes 723 and 723A (Aldgate–Tilbury Ferry). They entered service on 1 July 1965, RCL2256 being seen at Aldgate bus station in the autumn of that year. This was one of the RCLs to be refurbished at Aldenham in 1980, repainted in red livery to work on Central Area route 149. While working on this route it received a rear-end shunt, resulting in its being fitted with a standard Routemaster platform. Sold in 1985 to join a fleet of standard RMs working for Southend Transport, it now resides in sunny Spain, belonging to an unknown owner. *Colin Brown*

In June 1965 Romford garage (RE) received 29 new RCLs to replace RTs on Green Line routes 721 and 722. Shortly after entering service, RCL2223 passes Roneo Corner, Romford, *en route* for Upminster. Compare this view with the picture of the same vehicle in later life, on page 57. *Bruce Jenkins*

In September 1966, in an experiment which sought to reduce engine noise, RM738 was fitted with a very ugly radiator grille, in which form it is seen at Flamstead End, working from Edmonton garage on route 279, on 9 September. Noise reduction proved to be minimal, and the modifications adversely affected the cooling system, so — thankfully — the experiment was deemed a failure. *Gerald Mead*

Norbiton garage (NB) provided nine RMs on route 14 (Kingston–Hornsey Rise), shared with Holloway and Putney, on Sundays and Bank Holiday Mondays — the only time one could travel by bus between Kingston and Central London without changing at Putney. Norbiton's RM1207 is seen in Gower Street, near Euston, on Whit Monday (30 May) 1966. *Gerald Mead*

In December 1962 Stockwell (SW) received its first new Routemasters (starting with RM1342), the garage being allocated 22 to replace RTLs on its share of route 37. It gained further RMs (for routes 2 and 88) from Putney in 1966/7, when the latter's routes 14 and 74 were converted to RML operation. RM1691 is seen on route 88 at Belmont on 26 May 1969. One of a large number of RMs to be withdrawn from service in September 1986, it moved thereafter to Scotland to start a new life with Strathtay Scottish and passing into preservation in 1990. *Gerald Mead*

Victoria garage's RM43 arrives at Hammersmith Butterwick bus station in 1968, looking very smart after receiving its second overhaul. Externally, various differences are apparent from its condition as built in 1959, notably the overpanelling of the offside route-number box and the brake-cooling grilles in the front wings. *Colin Brown*

Derby Day was (and is) always a very busy day for the 406F bus route, which takes racegoers from Epsom station up the hill to the racecourse at Epsom Downs. Operation in June 1967 saw RTs working alongside Routemasters. Godstone-allocated RML2319, then just under two years old, is seen arriving at the racecourse with a full load. This would be one of the few unlucky RMLs which, having completed their stint with London Country in the 1970s, never re-entered service following their return to London Transport, being stripped for spares and sent for scrap almost immediately. *Roy Hobbs*

The only provincial customer for new Routemasters was the Northern General Transport Co, based at Gateshead, which placed an order for 50. Modelled on RMF1254, they were to be 30ft long with a forward entrance. They were delivered in two batches, 18 in the first (numbered 2085-2102) and 32 in the second (2103-34), all being in service by the middle of 1965. Featured here is 2120 (FPT 590C), seen crossing the Tyne Bridge in Newcastle on route 42 to Crook in 1967. This bus remained in service with the company until December 1980, whereafter it was sent to a breaker at Rotherham and thence to a dealer at Cheam. It managed to avoid being scrapped, however, passing in August 1986 to Stagecoach of Perth and later being used on that company's Magic Bus routes in Glasgow. By September 1992 it had finally settled down to preservation in Sidcup. *Frank Mussett*

Northern General Routemaster 2109, seen on Newcastle–Middlesbrough route 55 in Stockton High Street (renowned as the longest in Britain) when just a few months old in May 1966. Renumbered 3093 in 1975, this bus would have its life cut short by a serious accident in October 1976, becoming the first of its type to be withdrawn by the company. *Gerald Mead*

The Northern General Routemasters

Despite AEC's efforts to elicit provincial orders for the Routemaster, the only customer for the type outside London was BET subsidiary Northern General Transport. Northern had, in fact, been an early customer for Leyland's revolutionary rear-engined Atlantean, but, disillusioned by that model's dubious reliability record, decided in 1963 to order 18 Routemasters. These were 30ft-long, forward-entrance buses, similar to RMF1254 but with Leyland O.600 engines; arriving between March and May 1964 as 2085-2102 (RCN 685-702), they were followed between November 1964 and June 1965 by 32 more, as 2103-34 (DUP 249B, EUP 404-7B, FPT 578-604C). Delivered in Northern's livery of dark red with cream waistband, they were put to work on the company's principal trunk routes linking Newcastle with Crook, Darlington (via Durham), West Hartlepool (via Chester-le-Street), Middlesbrough and Sunderland. In December 1966 Northern acquired a 51st Routemaster in the shape of RMF1254 itself (its operation in LT service having been blocked by the TGWU), suitably re-engined with a Leyland O.600 unit, repainted in NGT red and numbered 2145. In 1969 some of Northern's Routemasters received a revised livery including more cream, which many felt improved their appearance, but repaints subsequently reverted to the earlier style.

In 1972 the desire to eliminate crew working prompted Northern to rebuild accident-damaged Routemaster 2085 as the 'Wearsider', with driving position set back to facilitate pay-as-you-enter operation. The availability of New Bus Grant ensured this conversion remained unique, but it nevertheless continued in service until 1978. By this time a renumbering scheme (implemented in 1975) had seen the Northern Routemasters adopt new identities, as 3069-3118 and 3129. Livery-wise, most had now donned NBC poppy red, the exception being 3109, which, along with 3071, had in 1975 been repainted in NBC's interpretation of Tyne & Wear PTE yellow and white.

Normal withdrawals of Northern Routemasters began in 1978 (accident victim 3093 having succumbed in 1976) and were completed by the end of 1980. London Transport's desire for second-hand Routemasters did not confine itself to London Country buses, and in 1979 a dozen of the Northern buses journeyed south to become RMF2761-72; however, none was used in service with LT, the vehicles in question being either dismantled for spares or sold on. Nevertheless, a number of Northern Routemasters were to see further service, some in Scotland with Stagecoach and others (paradoxically) on sightseeing work in London, in LT livery, some converted to open-top. At the time of writing (July 2004) three remain in London service with the Big Bus Company, three (in addition to RMF1254) survive in preservation, while yet others are still extant in non-PSV use, both in the UK and overseas.

In 1969 13 of Northern's Routemasters were treated to an attractive livery with more cream than used hitherto, 2111 (FPT 581C) being seen so adorned at Chester-le-Street. Subsequent repaints were to the original style, albeit with the revised (lower-case) fleetname shown here. *Kevin Lane*

The BEA airport Routemasters

Towards the end of 1966 a fleet of 65 forward-entrance Routemasters was constructed for British European Airways (BEA) for use on the LT-operated service from West London Air Terminal in Gloucester Road to Heathrow Airport, then the preserve of the 1½-deck AEC Regal IV coaches. The Routemasters were ordered on the strength of successful trials carried out with RMF1254 and its luggage trailer. The fleet took eight months to construct and was numbered by LT as BEA1-65. The buses sported BEA's livery of blue and white with black waistband and wheels. Late in 1969 the airline adopted a new livery of orange and white, and by 1972 its entire Routemaster fleet had donned these colours. However, following the merger of BEA and BOAC as British Airways (BA), there was another change of livery, and Routemasters started to receive navy blue and white.

By 1975 the airport service had been rationalised, and the Gloucester Road terminal ceased to function as a check-out point. As a result 13 Routemasters were rendered surplus to requirements, and these vehicles were purchased by LT, which renumbered them as RMA1-13. Various modifications were carried out to make them suitable for stage-carriage work, including the installation of bell-cord and bell-pushes, the removal of luggage racks and the fitting of slipboard-holders under the front canopy. These RMAs entered service in October 1975 from Romford's North Street (NS) garage on route 175 (Dagenham–North Romford) but lasted in service for less than a year, due to trade-union complaints regarding the absence of grab-rails. A few were subsequently converted for driver-training duties, with staircase removed and a seat for the instructor fixed directly behind the driver.

Further reductions in the airport service resulted in LT's purchasing another 14 BA Routemasters; then, some 15 months after the opening of the Piccadilly Line extension from Hounslow West to Heathrow (in December 1977), LT purchased the remainder of the fleet. Several were duly repainted in LT red, complete with bullseye motif, but most initially retained BA blue and white, working staff-bus services to Aldenham Works from garages around London, while others joined the training fleet.

With the closure of Aldenham in 1986, withdrawals became inevitable. In 1987 six joined the Original London Sightseeing Tour fleet, being used from Battersea garage on tours and charter work, complete with proper blind-boxes, while others found employment with private operators, several being shipped abroad.

One of BEA's fleet of forward-entrance Routemasters, BEA27 waits to leave Heathrow Airport for the West London Air Terminal in March 1968. Ten years later, in 1978, it would be purchased by LT, becoming RMA37 and being used as an Aldenham Works staff bus. Now owned by Timebus Travel, it is often seen around London in pristine condition on wedding hires. *Colin Brown*

Having arrived on route 76 from Tottenham, FRM1 lays over in the bus station at Victoria in December 1967. Damaged by an engine fire in August, the bus had not long returned to service following repair, during which most of its original, non-opening windows were replaced by the conventional quarter-drop type seen here. *Colin Brown*

FRM1

In 1964 AEC designers had begun work on what was to be the ultimate development of the Routemaster theme — a rear-engined, front-entrance double-decker suitable for one-person operation. However, by the time the prototype first saw the light of day the project had turned out to be still-born; Leyland had recently taken over AEC and had no desire to develop a rival to its own Atlantean model, while London Transport seemed more interested in following the Continental example of operation with high-capacity single-deckers. Nevertheless, FRM1 was taken into stock in July 1966, finally entering service some 12 months later, from Tottenham garage, on routes 34B and 76. It was originally fitted with a thermostatically controlled system of heating and ventilation and so lacked opening windows, but this was not particularly successful in operation. In August 1967

its service life was halted by an engine fire, which required firemen to break windows in order to allow smoke to escape, and in the course of the ensuing works visit opening windows were fitted. In 1969 the bus was converted for one-person operation and reallocated to Croydon, ostensibly for single-vehicle route 233 but in practice also working alongside Atlanteans on the 234B. Following overhaul in March 1973 it moved to another single-bus route — the 284 — from Potters Bar, where it was treated very gingerly. Despite this, in 1976 it was involved in an accident which necessitated its return to Chiswick Works. By now its stage-carriage career was over; following repair it began a new life on the Round London Sightseeing Tour, based at Stockwell garage, where it remained until withdrawal in 1983. This unique bus is now preserved at London's Transport Museum.

3

The 1970s

THE first day of the decade brought about the greatest change to London Transport since its creation in 1933: the splitting of LT between the erstwhile Central Area (red) and Country Area (green) operations. Control of the 'red' bus routes was transferred to the Greater London Council (GLC) in a move which amounted to de-nationalisation, while the green bus routes, along with the Green Line coach services, were handed over to a National Bus Company subsidiary, London Country Bus Services Ltd (LCBS). In one fell swoop LT lost 209 Routemasters, comprising the entire coach fleet of RMCs and RCLs together with 97 green RMLs (three having been exchanged for Leyland Atlanteans). By the end of the decade, however, virtually all of these would be reacquired by LT, apart from RML2423/4, which had been broken up, and a few which remained with LCBS into early 1980 before returning to LT (and RMC4, formerly CRL4, which LCBS retained).

At the end of the 1960s the future of the Routemaster had looked bleak, as new single- and double-deck buses designed for one-person operation (OPO) began to be delivered. Yet in the early 1970s only a handful of standard RMs had been withdrawn, all but one being the victims of accidents or fires. The first to be withdrawn was RM304 following accident damage, to be followed by three more in 1972 (RMs 1268, 1447 and 1659) as a result of arson. Two more RMs suffered fire damage in 1973 (RMs 50 and 1368) and were withdrawn, but the latter was resurrected as a single-decker for experimental use. The exception was the withdrawal in September 1972 of five-year-old RML2691, sold to a cosmetics company for promotion work overseas. Otherwise London's Routemaster fleet remained intact throughout the 1970s; indeed, it was expanded through second-hand purchases made necessary by the extreme unreliability of the new OPO buses and an acute shortage of spare parts (including those for Routemasters).

Meanwhile, following the repainting of RM1737 in 1969 as an all-over advertisement (which had created a mild sensation rather than an adverse reaction), LT saw an opportunity to earn some extra income by having 25 RMLs similarly treated between 1971 and 1974. Thereafter the novelty wore off, and LT decided to discontinue all-over advertising, bar a few exceptions.

London Country also climbed on the bandwagon by painting three RMCs as all-over advertisements, starting in 1972. The same year also marked a change to a lighter green to replace the old LT Lincoln green, but six months later LCBS was forced to abandon its own livery in favour of corporate NBC leaf green, the first Routemaster to be so treated appearing in October.

The year 1972 also witnessed the first signs of LCBS disenchantment with Routemasters, several RMCs and RCLs being removed from Green Line duty and demoted to bus use. This began a trend which quickly saw the removal of all Routemasters from Green Line routes, and which, later in the decade, would see the gradual replacement of Routemasters in general, mainly due to the cost of crew operation, particularly on sparsely used routes.

LT's first opportunity to increase its Routemaster fleet arose in 1975, when it purchased 13 such vehicles surplus to the needs of British Airways (formerly BEA), these buses being classified RMA; by the end of the decade it had acquired all 65, British Airways withdrawing its last examples in March 1979. Meanwhile RM8, the first production Routemaster, dating from 1959, entered service for the first time in 1976. Towards the end of 1977 the first LCBS Routemasters became available; then, right at the end of the decade, LT bought 12 ex-Northern General Routemasters, re-creating the RMF class (numbered RMF2761-72 to follow the last RMLs) but in the event never using them. LT also had the opportunity in the early 1980s to buy more ex-Northern General Routemasters but declined because they were too non-standard and the pressure to obtain as many Routemasters as possible had receded, as the chapter on the 1980s will explain.

Although the latter half of the 1970s saw an end to most all-over advertising liveries, there was still variety in the Routemaster fleet as LT created some special liveries of its own: 25 RMs (temporarily redesignated SRMs) painted silver in 1977 to mark HM The Queen's Silver Jubilee and, in 1979, 12 RMs adorned in 'Shillibeer' livery and another 16 in red-and-yellow 'Shoplinker' livery. Added to this were various trainers and staff buses on the streets of London still wearing LCBS green or British Airways blue and white, until such time as LT got around to repainting them.

Contrary to predictions, the 1970s had turned out to be a very good decade for LT's Routemaster fleet, which, instead of contracting, had actually expanded. The RT class had finally been withdrawn from passenger service and, in some cases, been replaced by Routemasters rather than by OPO vehicles. Better still for the Routemasters was that LT's next priority was replacement of the singularly unsuccessful DMS fleet; by the end of 1979 the GLC had finally to admit that 100% OPO was neither practicable nor desirable and that the Routemaster fleet should be retained in preference to replacement by modern, doored, crew-operated buses. The future for the London Routemaster in the 1980s looked bright.

RM1237 began its service life in December 1962, allocated to Tottenham garage. This view at Clapham Common, while the bus was working from Chalk Farm garage (CF) on route 45, was recorded in September 1970, soon after its second Aldenham Works overhaul. By this time the gold fleetname was non-underlined. Note also that the RM is carrying both bonnet and radiator badges. A later view of this bus in a very different guise appears on page 54. *Iain MacGregor*

Below left: The idea of all-over advertising on London's buses first arose in 1969, when the Silexine paint company held a competition among its executives to design a suitable livery. The company then persuaded London Transport to apply the winning design, depicting guardsmen marching against a background of well-known London landmarks, to a bus for a trial period of operation. RM1737 was chosen, entering service thus on 14 August 1969 from Riverside garage (R) in Hammersmith on route 11 and later moving to Mortlake (M) for route 9. There were very mixed feelings about this development, but it boosted revenue at the rate of £1,000 a month per bus, and between 1969 and 1976 a total of 21 RMs and six RMLs had all-over advertising liveries applied. RM1737 is seen at the Shepherd's Bush terminus of the 11. *Colin Brown*

Below right: The second RM to receive an all-over advertisement was RM971 (for Yellow Pages), which entered service on 18 April 1971 on route 11 from Dalston garage, where it remained for seven months. In November 1971 it moved to Stockwell for routes 2 and 88, on which it worked until 10 March 1972, when it was taken out of service for repainting; on 29 March it reappeared in a second version of Yellow Pages livery, thereafter working solely from Dalston garage, again on route 11, until 27 April 1973. This picture, taken at Liverpool Street station, shows the vehicle carrying the first style of livery shortly after entering service thus in April 1971. *Colin Brown*

In June 1969 the BEA airport Routemasters started to receive a new livery of orange and white with black wheels, but the general consensus was that this cheapened their appearance. This picture shows BEA4 at the West London Air Terminal in Gloucester Road, just after receiving its new livery in June 1970, at which time many of the luggage trailers were still in their original blue. In June 1979 BEA4 was purchased by London Transport and became RMA30. After a spell working as an Aldenham Works staff bus, the vehicle was withdrawn in August 1987 and scrapped. *Colin Brown*

A new London Transport logo appeared in 1971 in the form of an 'open' bullseye motif with LT's name inserted. The first vehicles to display this symbol were the new OPO Daimler Fleetlines, followed by some of the Routemaster fleet, albeit in a different offside position. This is demonstrated by RM1072, surrounded by RFs and an AEC Swift on the Staines West stand while working from Hounslow on route 117 in March 1972. This RM would leave the British Isles to set sail for Canada in 1990 and is now working for Duke of Kent Bus Tours in Ontario. *Colin Brown*

The third Routemaster to appear in an all-over advertising livery was RML2702, for Spiller's Home Pride bread. As such it entered service on route 15 from Upton Park in July 1971, moving to Holloway for route 14 two months later, but this was a very short-lived livery, lasting only until October 1971. The bus is pictured passing King's Cross on route 14 just before its removal from service. *Bruce Jenkins*

The livery for Bertorelli Continental ice cream, as applied to RM2140, was another very colourful example of all-over advertising. The bus carried this livery for just over a year, from 20 June 1972 until 9 July 1973, during which time it worked from four different garages — Battersea (for route 22), Stockwell (route 88), Finchley (26 and Sunday 2B) and finally Streatham (159 and Sunday 59). It is seen freshly into service in June 1972 at the Putney Common terminus of route 22. *Harry Luff*

One of the most bizarre liveries was that for Younger's Tartan Beer applied to RML2701, which sported an all-over tartan scheme. It lasted 15 months (May 1972 to August 1973) in this condition, working from Upton Park, Holloway and Hackney garages. It was photographed in June 1972 on a Sunday working of route 15 to East Acton Lane. *Colin Brown*

Relegated to bus work by London Country once its Green Line days were over, RMC1516 sustained major roof damage in January 1972 after losing an argument with a low bridge and disappeared inside Aldenham (then still undertaking work for LCBS) for a new roof. Around this time the fashion for all-over advertising, all the rage in Central London, was spreading to the country, and RMC1516 duly reappeared in a multi-coloured livery for Welwyn Department Store, working from Hatfield garage on routes 341 and 341B. It is seen here in Welwyn on route 341B in November 1972. In May 1974, when the store was taken over by Fine Fare, RMC1516 was repainted in the latter's colours of blue and orange, in which form it spent its final few months working from St Albans garage on trunk route 330. Bought back by LT in 1977, it is now preserved in Norfolk. *Colin Brown*

In 1973 a further 12 LT Routemasters donned advertising liveries. One of these was RML2280, which was to become unique in receiving successive liveries to the order of two different advertisers. From March to October it promoted Hanimex Projectors, working initially from Chalk Farm garage and seen here freshly into service on route 24 at Pimlico in April; it later moved to Upton Park for use on routes 15 and 101. In November it received its second advert livery, for Myson, thereafter working entirely from Hackney on routes 6 and 30 until December 1975. *Colin Brown*

One could hardly fail to notice RM906, which in June 1973 appeared in a livery resembling a zebra to promote Barker & Dobson's Everton Mints. Retaining this scheme until March 1975, it worked mostly from Streatham garage on route 159 (and the 59 on Sundays) but also had spells at Hendon on routes 13 and 113 and Walworth on route 12. It is seen on layover at West Hampstead on a Sunday working of the 59 in June 1974. *Colin Brown*

Resting between journeys on route 27, RMs 380 and 436 of Holloway (HT) garage lay over in Adelaide Road, Teddington, one Saturday in September 1972. This was a time when bus routes still ran right across London from one side to the other, the 27 linking Teddington, in West London, with Highgate, in North London.
Iain MacGregor

Approaching the end of its career as a Green Line coach working from Windsor garage, RMC1493 arrives at Hyde Park Corner on route 704 in April 1972. Relegated to bus work, it would later be transferred to Swanley garage for route 477, repainted in NBC leaf green, but still saw occasional use on Green Line work, notably on special events such as route 719 to Brands Hatch. Unfortunately this RMC didn't survive, being scrapped at Wombwell Diesels in 1981. *Colin Brown*

RCL2251 at Victoria in March 1972, during its last week of scheduled Green Line service, on route 704 from Dunton Green garage. Subsequently demoted to bus work, by 1978 it would be repurchased by LT. A surprise move in 1980 saw most of the surviving RCL fleet given a full overhaul at Aldenham Works, in which their doors and luggage racks were removed and their seats re-trimmed in blue moquette, and emerge in LT red; they then had a four-year stint in service on route 149 (Stamford Hill to Victoria). Its stay of execution at an end, RCL2251 would make its final journey to the breaker's yard in 1985. *Colin Brown*

Demoted to bus work from Reigate garage, RCL2229 is seen on route 430 in Sandcross Lane, Woodhatch, in April 1973. This was an isolated working, as the route was usually operated by Merlin single-deckers. Like the rest of its class, it would return to LT, visiting Aldenham Works for overhaul prior to putting in four years' Central Area bus work on route 149. Restored to original condition, it now resides at London's Transport Museum, as a prime example of its class. *Roy Hobbs*

New in September 1967, RML2691 began its career on route 207 from Hanwell garage, where it remained until September 1972. LT then made the surprising decision to sell this five-year-old bus before even its first overhaul, presumably in response to an irresistible offer from the purchaser, Gala Cosmetics International Ltd, best known for its Mary Quant brand.

After conversion by a Burnley-based company in 1973 the vehicle was shipped to Canada but returned to Britain occasionally; following further alterations, carried out at LPC Coachworks of Hounslow Heath, where this picture was taken in June 1975, it resumed its promotional work, which included a visit to Finland. In 1998 it was tracked down in Hillerstorp in southern Sweden, in red livery. In 2001 members of the Routemaster Operators & Owners Association went to inspect the bus with a view to buying it and shipping it back to the UK, but regrettably it was found to be in too poor a condition and shortly afterwards was destroyed by fire. *Colin Brown*

By the 1970s FRM1 had been reallocated to Croydon, but following overhaul in 1973 it returned to North London at Potters Bar, being seen in the latter town on its designated route, the single-bus 284, in 1975. *Harry Luff*

Nearly 13 years of RM1's life, from 1959 to 1972, were spent in the driver-training fleet, and it was during this time, on the occasion of its second overhaul, that its original-style bonnet assembly was changed for the standard version, as fitted to production RMs. In 1972 it was sold to the Lockheed Hydraulics Co of Leamington Spa, in whose ownership it is seen on trade plates at Hampton Court station in March 1974. In 1981 RM1 returned to London Transport ownership, based initially at Chiswick Works but transferred in 1982 to Aldenham for refurbishment by the apprentices. It now resides at London's Transport Museum. *Geoff Rixon*

Following accident damage Northern's first Routemaster was subjected to a drastic rebuild which saw the driving position moved backwards to permit one-man operation. Named *Wearsider*, 2085 (RCN 685) was outshopped in 1972 in an attractive red/white livery which pre-dated the introduction of NBC's corporate image later in the year. Seen at Jarrow on 9 September, it remained unique in this form but led a full service life, not being withdrawn until 1978, by which time it had been renumbered (as 3069) and succumbed to poppy red. *Kevin Lane*

With the introduction from 1972 of NBC's corporate image the majority of Northern's Routemaster fleet assumed poppy-red livery, but, like many other Northern vehicles based within the new county of Tyne & Wear, two were painted in the yellow used (albeit with a greater proportion of white) by Tyne & Wear PTE. Formerly 2087, 3071 (RCN 687) had been so renumbered early in 1975 and is pictured outside Sunderland depot in September of that year. *Charles Dean / Kevin Lane collection*

London Country's Leatherhead garage had an allocation of RMCs for the 406 (Redhill–Kingston), which route it shared with Reigate. RMC1464 is seen at Tattenham Corner against the backdrop of Epsom Racecourse in March 1976. The end for Routemasters on this route came in 1978, when many of the RMCs returned to London Transport for use as training buses. It was while thus employed that RMC1464 was involved in an accident which probably saved its life: roof damage led to its conversion to an open-top 'special events' vehicle, in which form it outlasted most of its sisters and is still in use today with Arriva, named 'Princess'. *Dave Brown*

The big event of 1977 was HM The Queen's Silver Jubilee, and to celebrate the event a fleet of 25 Routemasters, temporarily renumbered SRM1-25, were painted in silver livery, the vehicles in question being chosen at random as they were passing through Aldenham Works for overhaul. LT really went to town, as internally these vehicles were fitted with plush 100%-wool 'EllR'-design carpeting, but sponsors were found to advertise on these vehicles, to fund the project. Their first appearance was at the Battersea Easter Parade in April, and all operated throughout the summer, the last finishing by the end of November. SRM17 (RM1894) is illustrated here working from Willesden garage on route 52 at Hyde Park Corner on 11 April 1977, during its first week in service. *Colin Brown*

Another of the Silver Jubilee fleet was Leyland-engined SRM3 (RM1650), seen in New Oxford Street on route 25 in the summer of 1977. In 1986 this would become one of the large number of Routemasters sold off to provincial operators, joining Blackpool Transport, where it remained until stored in 1994. Another operator that was starting to accumulate a Routemaster fleet around this time was Reading Mainline, which in 1997 acquired RM1650, placing it in service that September. By 1999 Reading Mainline was being wound down, having been taken over by municipally owned Reading Buses, and RM1650 was sold to a dealer in Bolton in February 2000. By this time, however, the Routemaster was back in favour in London, and RM1650 was one of a number repurchased by Transport for London, to be completely refurbished throughout by Marshall's of Cambridge and fitted with new Cummins engines and fully automatic gearboxes. RM1650 joined the First London fleet in Dcecember 2001, being allocated to Westbourne Park for routes 7 and 23, and was one of the 15 Routemasters to don gold livery in 2002 for HM The Queen's Golden Jubilee, temporarily reverting to its 'silver' fleetnumber of SRM3. *Dave Brown*

RML2460 was numerically the last of the Country Area Routemasters. By now in NBC leaf green, it was photographed in the village of Harefield on 3 September 1977, working for London Country from Hemel Hempstead Two Waters (HH) garage on route 347A. Shared with Garston garage (GR) in Watford, this was the last crew-operated route in London Country's Northern Area and had only a year left before OPO conversion. Note the unusual indicator on the nearside front wing. Just three months after the picture was taken RML2460 would be back in LT hands, allocated to Holloway. Refurbished in the early 1990s and fitted with a Cummins engine, it went to work for Leaside Buses at Tottenham; a further decade on, in September 2003, still working from the same garage (by now Arriva-controlled), it met with a bad accident and was subsequently dismantled for spares. *Colin Brown*

Routemaster coach RCL2244 started life in June 1965 allocated to Romford (RE) garage on Green Line routes 721 and 722. Soon after passing to London Country Bus Services in 1970 the RCLs were relegated to bus work, RCL2244 being reallocated to Dorking (DS) to work the long and busy 414 (Dorking–Croydon), shared with Reigate garage. By 1974 difficulties in obtaining spares for the Routemasters saw many laid up unfit for service; however, by this time a programme was underway to repaint the RCLs in corporate NBC leaf green, and RCL2244 suffered the indignity of being towed engineless to Leatherhead garage for repainting! The bus eventually returned to service, remaining on the 414 until October 1977, when most of the Routemasters were replaced, but RCL2244 stayed on at Dorking as that garage's sole surviving RCL, working chiefly on route 448 but seen here in Dorking on route 449 on 30 March 1978. Finally withdrawn by LCBS later in 1978, it then returned to LT and, like most other members of its class, was refurbished (in 1980) for Central Area work on route 149. This use continued until November 1982, when it was sold to dealer North's at Sherburn-in-Elmet (near Leeds), to be scapped in 1983. *Colin Brown*

RML2744, allocated to Stonebridge
Park, passes through Wembley on
route 18 in the summer of 1978,
just a few months before the
route's Routemasters were replaced
by crew-operated Fleetlines.
Stonebridge Park garage too would
not be around for much longer,
closing its doors as an operational
base on 15 August 1981. RML2744
worked latterly for London United
from Shepherds Bush garage on
routes 9 and 94, but the 94 forsook
its Routemasters for low-floor
vehicles in January 2004.
Geoff Rixon

By 1979 all the British Airways
Routemaster services had ceased
to operate. LT eventually purchased
all 65 vehicles, numbering them as
RMA1-65 — albeit in order of
acquisition rather than to match
their registrations. The first few
entered service from Romford's
North Street garage on route 175,
having had a few modifications
carried out but looking shabby still
in faded orange and white.
The other RMAs worked as staff
buses, ferrying employees to/from
Aldenham Works, or as trainers;
staff bus RMA1 (ex-BEA21), seen
here inside the old Hammersmith
garage in December 1978, was the
first to receive LT red with white
bullseye. This vehicle is now
preserved in Cambridge.
Geoff Rixon

On 31 December 1973 RM1368, then working
from Tottenham garage, had its upper deck
gutted by fire as a result of an arson attack.
Initial plans for a full repair were shelved
in favour of rebuilding as a single-decker,
whereafter the bus was allocated to Chiswick
Works as an experimental vehicle, finally
releasing RM8 for normal service in 1976.
Pictured at Syon Park in September 1978,
RM1368 has been in preservation since 1990.
Colin Brown

'Shillibeers' on parade: the launch of the fleet of RMs at the City of London's Guildhall on 2 March 1979, with seven of the 12 vehicles on view. Each was sponsored by a different advertiser. The second vehicle in the line-up, RM2208, is now preserved in this livery and resides at Dewsbury Bus Museum in Yorkshire. *Geoff Rixon*

Another view of a 'Shillibeer', this time in service. Working from Wandsworth garage (WD), RM2130 passes through Notting Hill on route 28 from Golders Green on 22 September 1979. The advertising contracts for the fleet had expired by November, but one bus remained in unsponsored Shillibeer livery until the early 1980s, working from Tottenham garage (AR) on route 41. RM2130's end would come in June 1987, when it was sold to breakers in Barnsley. *Geoff Rixon*

Freshly into service in April 1979 as one of the Shoplinker fleet of 16 Routemasters, RM2189, seen leaving the Park Lane stand, displays prominent advertising for its 30p fare which some members of the public took to mean route 30! The service was short-lived, but RM2189 would remain in service from Stockwell garage until withdrawn in March 1993, whereupon it was sold to a breaker at Carlton in Yorkshire. *Geoff Rixon*

Northern General 2095 (RCN 695) was first licensed for passenger service in April 1964 but is seen here some 15 years later at Lanchester Village, near Consett, in NBC poppy red, as applied from 1972. The Northern fleet had been renumbered in January 1975, the Routemasters becoming 3069-3118/29; RCN 695 was now 3079. Normal withdrawals had begun in May 1977, and by April 1979, when this picture was taken, only 18 remained in service; by the end of the following year all would be gone, the majority to the scrapyard. In the case of 3079, however, there was a sad twist to the tale: purchased for preservation in January 1981, it was restored to Northern red and cream but in 1986 was moved to the Stagecoach company's garage in Perth (where its owners were employed), but in 1987 both bus and garage were destroyed by fire. Happily, 14 Northern Routemasters are believed to survive; of these, five (including ex-LT RMF1254) are in preservation, and three are still in service in London with the Big Bus Company. *Dave Brown*

A view typical of what one would see when visiting LT's bus-overhaul works at Aldenham; taken in September 1979, it shows RM545 in need of a complete new front end following a severe accident. Fitted with a DAF engine (in 1988), it would end up working for London Coaches and, later, Arriva on the Original London Sightseeing Tour. It is now owned by Mediabus of Croydon. *Harry Luff*

Above: A very smart RM1688, based at Clapton garage, passes through Old Street, Shoreditch, on route 22 (Hackney–Putney Common) in August 1980, in the days when routes ran right across Central London. The future was bleak for RM1688, as it was broken up at Rotherham in December 1983. *Geoff Rixon*

Left: Late in 1979 a solitary RM appeared on the road in an all-over advertisement livery for Wisdom, celebrating 200 years of the toothbrush. RM1237 worked on various routes across Central London, being seen here at Mornington Crescent while working from Palmers Green garage on route 29 (Enfield–Victoria). This RM would be one of the early withdrawals, being dismantled in December 1983 by Booth's of Rotherham. *Geoff Rixon*

Fresh from overhaul, RM2195 passes through Hornchurch bound for Barking on route 193 on 15 September 1979. Seven Kings garage (AP), where it is allocated, had received its first RMs as recently as 1977, to replace its RTs, but by 1984 the Routemasters would themselves give way to new OPO Leyland Titans. RM2195 would be sold in March 1988 to United Counties, not to enter service but to provide spares for that company's fleet of similar buses, being scrapped at Kettering by June 1989. *Geoff Rixon*

Working on route 7, Middle Row-based RM144 manœuvres into the Edgware Road at Marble Arch in June 1978. New with plain, non-opening windows at the front of its upper deck, this bus has received a later body, of the style fitted from new to RM254 onwards. Bodies and subframes were separated during overhaul at Aldenham Works, and rarely did a bus regain its original body. RM144 would receive one more overhaul, in the 1980s, thereafter working from West Ham garage until withdrawal (in 1985) and a one-way journey to breakers at Carlton. *Geoff Rixon*

4

The 1980s

AS THE decade dawned, LT's vehicle problems were starting to abate. The newest buses to be delivered, MCW Metrobuses (M class) and Leyland Titans (T class), were operating quite successfully. Also, the influx of ex-LCBS RMLs, which were immediately painted red, helped towards the re-conversion of some routes back to Routemaster operation in the interests of improved reliability and (in the case of some of the busier routes converted unsuccessfully to OPO) to speed up loadings. Such was LT's enthusiasm for the Routemaster at this time that the surviving RCLs (apart from cinema bus RCL2221), hitherto employed on staff-bus and driver-training duties, were modified for passenger use in Central London by the removal of doors, luggage racks etc, the first entering service in August 1981.

Returning to the non-LT Routemasters, the final London Country buses ran in March 1980, and Northern General withdrew its last example in December 1980. For the time being Routemaster operation would be confined to LT.

A high-point for the London Routemaster was reached during 1980 with the advent of the 'showbus' era; individual garages 'adopted' a bus for display purposes, normally restoring original features which had been removed and adding various embellishments. Such vehicles were always immaculately turned out and appeared on normal services when not attending shows or being titivated.

Another special livery appeared in 1981, this time to mark the wedding of Prince Charles and Lady Diana Spencer. Eight RMs operated between June and September/October in what was known colloquially as 'parcel' livery.

More colour-scheme changes were evident in 1983 to mark LT's Golden Jubilee; one Routemaster (RM1983) was painted in gold livery and four more in pseudo-1933 livery, while others had minor livery changes. Sadly, during the following year an edict was issued by management stating that all buses should be in standard livery; modified liveries were outlawed, and the 'showbus' era effectively drew to a close.

The year 1982 marked an unexpected turning-point for the Routemaster fleet in London, arising from a judgement by the House of Lords in December 1981 upholding an appeal by the London Borough of Bromley against LT's 'Fares Fair' policy of reducing bus fares. The massive increase in passenger numbers which this policy had created was halted and, as fares doubled, a massive decrease occurred. Services were cut, and crew operation reduced to save costs. Suddenly the RM fleet became vulnerable, and in the second half of the year the first standard RMs (apart from the handful of accident victims and some second-hand buses which LT had found to be beyond redemption) were withdrawn. In 1982 some 150 were either sold or broken up, generally (in the interests of standardisation) those with Leyland engines. Very few of these early withdrawals saw further service, but later in the decade, as more and more RMs became surplus, their appeal to both British and overseas buyers was almost irresistible. For British operators the RM was a useful tool in winning passengers as deregulation (in 1986) opened up new opportunities. However, the euphoria had already subsided in some areas by the end of the decade, when the first provincial withdrawals occurred.

The 1980s brought dramatic changes not only to London's Routemaster fleet but also to London Transport itself, which ceased to exist on 29 June 1984 following re-nationalisation and the creation of a new body, London Regional Transport (LRT). Removed from the GLC and placed under direct Government control, it seemed likely to be subject to a much stricter regime, with OPO extended and crew-operated RMs withdrawn. In addition, revenue subsidies would be cut and bus services put out to competitive tender.

At the end of 1984 the last RCLs were withdrawn from public service, notwithstanding the costly modifications carried out only three years previously to make them suitable for bus work. In March 1985 RCL2249 was handed over to the London Transport Museum, joining the unique FRM1, withdrawn two years earlier; later in the decade RM1 and RM2 would be added to the collection.

The year 1985 saw more organisational changes as LRT's bus operations were transferred to a newly created subsidiary, London Buses Ltd. On the operational front OPO was driving the Routemasters out of the suburbs, and their withdrawal continued relentlessly. By this time provincial operators, some of which had previously abandoned crew operation, were taking an interest in London's surplus RMs. A considerable number went to Scotland, in a trend started by Stagecoach in January 1985, while others entered service abroad in such disparate locations as Sri Lanka, Niagara Falls and Hong Kong. Further economies were introduced in the latter years of the 1980s as bus overhauls were contracted out or undertaken at garages and the famous Aldenham and Chiswick works were closed down.

By 1989 the Routemaster fleet in the ownership of London Buses had diminished to some 500 standard RMs, 39 RMCs, 11 RCLs and 15 RMAs, but the RML fleet was largely intact. Furthermore, the wheel of fortune was turning once more in the Routemaster's favour. In the previous year (1988) LRT had announced that no more routes would be converted to OPO. This meant that the remaining 25 Routemaster-operated routes were likely to survive well into the next decade, and serious consideration was being given to updating the remaining

By 1980 the specially liveried RMs of the previous year had all been repainted, except for RM1237, the Wisdom Toothbrush bus, but there was a highlight to come later in the year. In August the RCL class was reinstated to work route 149 from Stamford Hill and Edmonton garages, having received overhauls at Aldenham Works in which their luggage racks and rear platform doors were removed and their plush seating was reupholstered in new blue moquette. Ex-works RCL2222 is seen arriving at Liverpool Street station on Sunday 9 August 1980, its first day of service on the 149. *Geoff Rixon*

vehicles, with trialling of new engines, modernised lighting etc.

The decade ended with yet more organisational changes. On 1 April 1989 responsibility for the operation of London Buses was transferred from London Buses Ltd to 11 new subsidiary companies as a prelude to deregulation of bus services in London during the next decade. Two of the companies revived the names of London General and London United and painted a few RMs in pseudo-pre-1933 liveries.

Finally, against all the odds, the RMC class was resurrected for passenger service when seven were used to operate a new express commuter route numbered X15. The vehicles looked splendid with their gold central and window relief and gold lettering. Unfortunately their moment of glory was brief, because the route was converted to OPO in 1991.

Once again, the Routemaster's prospects in London looked favourable for the following decade. Furthermore, for the first time it was now possible to travel on Routemasters in several towns and cities around Britain and abroad.

Bound for the Mansion House, refurbished RCL2223 of Stamford Hill garage arrives at Liverpool Street on 12 August 1980, its fourth day in service. This vehicle was one of the lucky survivors: having completed its stint on the 149 in September 1984 it was sold in April 1985 to dealer E. Brakell of Cheam; eventually, in April 1988, it was re-sold to a company at Raynes Park which converted it to a luxury hospitality vehicle (tables and table-lamps being fitted at Aldenham Works), and a few years later it passed in a similar capacity to a company in Farnham, Surrey. By 2002 it had been sold on to Heathrow Airport Ltd as a mobile publicity vehicle for the new Terminal 5. *Geoff Rixon*

Walthamstow bus station forms the backdrop for this 1980s picture of West Ham garage's RM199 departing for Chingford on route 69. This RM had been allocated to West Ham when new in February 1960 but would end its career at Camberwell in December 1987 before heading for the breaker's yard in January 1988. *Geoff Rixon*

Another very smart Routemaster fresh from overhaul is RM600, a New Cross bus, on the Camberwell New Road on route 171 on a fine April day in 1980. It should be noted that the vehicle has the early-style body with plain front windows on the upper deck, as originally fitted to Routemasters up to RM253. RM600's LT career continued until June 1992, after which it was sold and shipped abroad to Matsuyama City, Ehime, Japan. *Geoff Rixon*

What Sunday afternoons in Croydon looked like in May 1980, in the years before the introduction of Sunday shopping. RM15, here working route 119B from Bromley garage (TB), would complete 32 years in service before being scrapped in 1992. *Geoff Rixon*

Photographed from the top deck of an RM travelling in the opposite direction, Palmers Green-based RM2123 arrives at the Silver Street, Edmonton, stop outside Pymmes Park on route 102, on a short working to Edmonton, Park Road (instead of terminating at Chingford station), on 30 October 1980. The offside illuminated advertising panel — a new development for London — was introduced in July 1964 and applied to nearly 200 RMs being built at this time and subsequently to 100 RMLs. However, the feature was later abandoned due to a lack of interest from advertisers. RM2123 displays plain panels following the discontinuation of the illuminated advertisements, but in later years normal advertisements would be pasted on the outside. The bus was scrapped in 1985. *Geoff Rixon*

A sight that will never be seen again: some of the Routemaster training-bus fleet, including a mixture of red and green RMs, RMLs and RMCs, lined up by the famous skid-pan at Chiswick Works, where they were based, on a Sunday afternoon in February 1981. Opened in 1921, the works would be closed in September 1987 and the site vacated for redevelopment.
Geoff Rixon

With a significant amount of snow and slushy roads, January 1981 was not the best time for bus photography, but Kingston-allocated RM1179 was caught on the outskirts of Richmond, near Star & Garter Hill, heading for Chessington Zoo on route 65. By now the RM was nearing the end of its career; 18 months later it was withdrawn and sold to a breaker in Leicester but was finally scrapped at LT's Aldenham Works.
Geoff Rixon

It was well known that anyone who liked well-presented London buses need look no further than Mortlake garage, which operated a fleet of around 50 Routemasters for routes 9, 9A (on Sundays) and 33, as well as a small allocation on the 73. Proving the point about condition, RM1373, complete with chrome headlamp surrounds and front wheel trims, leaves Hammersmith Butterwick bus station on route 9A one Sunday in February 1981. The Mortlake fleet would be decimated a year later, following the decision to withdraw RMs fitted with Simms electrical equipment and Leyland engines, many of which had always been allocated there. RM1373 was dismantled and scrapped at Aldenham in June 1983 — around the time that Mortlake garage, which had had an allocation of RMs since 1962, closed its doors for good. *Geoff Rixon*

Following the launch of FRM1 in 1966, Chiswick Works began work on an even more advanced Routemaster design, codenamed XRM. This new bus, which, due to the increasing use of OPO vehicles in London, never progressed beyond mock-up stage, was intended to incorporate a new hydrostatic suspension system developed by Lockheed of Leamington. Trialled initially on RM1 during its period of ownership by Lockheed, the 'Active Ride Control' (ARC) system, as it was known, was transferred to RM116. This bus went into service with the new suspension in June 1980 at Mortlake garage on route 9 and also worked from Stamford Brook garage, which was conveniently close to Chiswick Works. When the XRM project was aborted RM116 was withdrawn, being sold for preservation in 1988. This view shows it at Hyde Park Corner, having just entered service on route 9 in June 1980. *Geoff Rixon*

In the summer of 1981 came another Royal occasion, the wedding of HRH The Prince of Wales and Lady Diana Spencer, which was to take place on 29 July at St Paul's Cathedral. This was a chance not to be missed for another special bus livery. The Routemaster was the only type selected, eight standard RMs being 'gift-wrapped' in red and silver livery. Duly nicknamed 'parcel buses', some were sponsored, while others carried in-house advertising. RM490 was the first to appear in this livery, as a test-bed, but never operated thus in service. On the day before the wedding crowds were immense, and a special service was operated along the procession route, with the RMs displaying special blinds. Pictured turning out of Oxford Street into Park Lane at Marble Arch on route 73, Hammersmith's RM534 had just entered service in its new livery in July 1981. Alas, its glory days would be short-lived; all eight wedding buses would be repainted in standard red by November that year, and RM534 scrapped in Yorkshire by 1985. *Geoff Rixon*

Wedding-liveried RM219, allocated to Camberwell garage, arrives at Ludgate Hill (near St Paul's Cathedral) on the one-day special service over the wedding-procession route on the day prior to the big event — Friday 28 July 1981 — displaying its special blinds for the day. The crowds in their hundreds visiting the event and all the bunting displayed on the buildings sets the mood for the occasion. RM219 would be withdrawn in 1985, leaving London with many others to join the Scottish Bus Group — in this case Clydeside Scottish, which operated services around the Paisley area. In 1989 RM219 was sold to Western Scottish and re-registered LDS 281A, but no more than a year later it was on the move again, to Kelvin Central Buses. This bus certainly had a wanderlust, as in 1993 it moved with nine other RMs to the South Coast resort of Bournemouth to join BHT Buses of Parkstone, where it was re-registered again, as YVS 291. After this operation finished in August 1994 the bus had brief spells with further UK owners before finally moving abroad to Warsaw, Poland. *Geoff Rixon*

LT's last new standard-length Routemaster built was RM2217, delivered in September 1965. When new, RM2210-7 differed from earlier RMs through having a grey band (instead of cream), a feature they shared with the red RMLs that followed them in production. However, both cream and grey had long since given way to white by the time RM2217 was photographed turning into Eden Street, Kingston, on route 281 from Fulwell garage in June 1981 — just a couple of weeks before RMs finished on this service. But RM2217 wasn't done yet and at the time of writing (July 2004) is still in service, working for Arriva from Brixton garage (BN) on routes 137 and 159. *Geoff Rixon*

The one-off experimental RMF1254, photographed after withdrawal by Northern General and return to the London area for preservation in March 1981. Still in full NBC poppy red, the bus is seen passing Parliament Square while on private-hire work on a hot July day in 1981. It now resides in Woodford, Essex. *Geoff Rixon*

Above: Following the doldrums of 1982 — a year to forget for RM enthusiasts, in view of the large number of withdrawals (mostly of Leyland-engined buses) — 1983 presented a much brighter picture. With London Transport celebrating its 50th anniversary, five Routemasters gained special liveries, RMs 8, 17, 1933 and 2116 receiving the very attractive 1933-style red and white with black lining, topped off with a silver roof, in which form they operated from several garages during the course of the year. RM17 is seen passing through Mill Hill on route 52 on 15 August 1983, shortly after entering service from Willesden (AC). In 1986 this bus would be one of the large number of RMs sold to SBG, joining the Clydeside Scottish fleet. It was re-registered LDS 214A in 1989, following transfer to Western Scottish, which by 1990 had sold it to a breaker. Luckily, however, it escaped the cutter's torch and is now preserved in Ipswich. *Geoff Rixon*

Top right: The fifth RM to be given a special livery for London Transport's 50th anniversary was, appropriately, RM1983, which was painted gold. This was definitely a bus one had to photograph in the sunshine — when one could catch up with it! — as it looked decidedly drab in dull conditions. Allocated to a number of garages whilst in gold. It is pictured turning into its then home garage of Thornton Heath on 30 April 1983, its first day of service on route 190. *Geoff Rixon*

Lower right: Another view of gold RM1983, here about to leave Hammersmith Broadway for Liverpool Street on route 9 from Ash Grove garage on 19 August 1983. The bus would revert to LT red in February 1984. Sold in September 1986 to Kelvin Scottish, it passed to Stagecoach one year later, joining Cumberland Motor Services at Carlisle, where it was one of eight RMs used on a cross-city service; five years later all were withdrawn and most placed in store, but RM1983 was sold to begin a new life abroad (see page 86). *Geoff Rixon*

Overall-advertisement buses reappeared late in 1983, when a pair of RMLs emerged in liveries for Lyle & Scott men's underwear. RML2412, promoting Jockey boxer shorts, worked from Putney garage on routes 14 and 22 and is pictured crossing Putney Bridge on 31 December. The other vehicle was RML2444, which carried a red/white scheme for Y-fronts and worked from Upton Park garage on route 15. *Geoff Rixon*

A third Routemaster to carry all-over advertising, in 1984, was RML2492, painted bright green and yellow to promote Underwood's photographic developing/printing service. Allocated to Ash Grove garage for routes 6 and 11, the bus is seen on a short working of the 6 to Marble Arch in July 1984. The controversy provoked by this garish scheme seemed to put a lid on all-over advertising on buses, and there would be no more in London until 2004. Fitted with a Cummins engine in 1990, RML2492 now keeps a lower profile, working for Arriva from Clapton garage (CT) on route 38. *Geoff Rixon*

Clydeside Scottish had the largest fleet of Routemasters owned by a provincial operator, acquiring more than 70, chiefly for services in the Paisley area, plus a further 25 for spares. The former RM550 is seen on an evening journey on route 639, passing through Paisley on its way to Johnstone in July 1986. This bus would pass in July 1988 to Western Scottish, being duly re-registered LDS 184A but spending only a year with that company before sale (via a London dealer) to a buyer in Germany. *Geoff Rixon*

In 1986 there was a positive development on the Routemaster front, when 50 were taken into Aldenham Works as part of a £250,000 programme to overhaul them for use on the Round London Sightseeing Tour, operated hitherto by Metrobuses. All received an attractive livery of red and cream, with gold underlined fleetnames and numbers. Now branded as 'The Original London Transport Sightseeing Tour', the tour was re-launched in May 1986. The sightseeing fleet was housed initially in the old Battersea garage (B), being joined later in the year by six RMAs made redundant from staff-bus duties by the closure of Aldenham Works, but in 1988 was transferred to Wandsworth (WD). Open-top RM658, seen about to turn into the centre bus lane on the tour route at Marble Arch in June 1986, would spend just under five years on this work before withdrawal and sale for scrap. *Geoff Rixon*

Refurbished for the sightseeing tour in 1986, RM644 was one of the 19 closed-top Routemasters used in the winter months or in inclement weather. This picture shows it crossing Lambeth Bridge soon after re-entering service in May 1986. In 1988 it too would be converted to open-top and three years later would be sold to Metroline Travel, being used in that company's Contract Services fleet at Cricklewood. As such it would be only ex-London Coaches open-top RM (as opposed to ERM) to be used by another company, all others being sold for scrap. It has since been fitted with RMC-style air-operated rear doors and, more recently, a Scania engine. *Geoff Rixon*

Blackpool Transport followed in the footsteps of the Scottish operators in purchasing withdrawn Routemasters from London Buses. In May 1986 six Leyland-engined RMs joined the fleet, painted in a very attractive red and white livery last used by Blackpool before World War 2. A further six arrived in April 1988, to be followed in 1989 by a solitary AEC-engined example which had been used by biscuit company Burton's. RM848, illustrated here arriving at Grange Park on route 5A in September 1986, was one of the first batch and was numbered 522 (later 422). The RMs never worked in the winter months, and by 1994 they never worked at all, having been placed in store. By that time Reading Mainline was amassing a fleet of Routemasters, and the Blackpool RMs duly made their way south. When Reading disposed of its fleet in 2000 the majority passed to London Bus Services Ltd; following refurbishment by Marshall's in 2001 RM848 joined London United at Shepherds Bush for routes 9 and 94. At the time of writing (July 2004) it was still going strong, albeit restricted to route 9, the 94 having been converted to operation with low-floor vehicles in February 2004. *Geoff Rixon*

Early in 1988 Stagecoach subsidiary United Counties purchased 12 Routemasters for use in Bedford and Corby, painting them in a livery of green with orange and yellow stripes and fitting each with a very smart 'Routemaster UC' triangular radiator badge. RM682 is seen on the outskirts of Bedford on route 101 in May 1988.

RM operation in Corby would cease in August 1991, while that in Bedford would last until the end of 1992. Re-registered as HVS 937 before sale in 1988, RM682 survives in the Netherlands. *Geoff Rixon*

At the start of its new life in Glasgow with Kelvin Scottish, RM419 arrives at Buchanan bus station in evening sunshine in July 1986. By the early 1990s its operator was experiencing financial difficulties, and Routemaster operation would cease in March 1993. Latterly registered EDS 393A, RM419 was sold to a Scottish dealer who in January 1995 sold it on to a breaker at Carlton in Yorkshire. *Geoff Rixon*

A gloomy scene depicting the fate that awaited Routemasters arriving at the breaker's yard. Photographed from the top deck of a similar bus, RM1044, withdrawn from Westbourne Park in September 1986, stands in the squelchy mud at Barnsley in February 1987. *Geoff Rixon*

The Barnsley breakers were surprised at the strength of the Routemaster's construction. With tangled metal strewn all around, erstwhile Forest District RM232, withdrawn in 1986, had just been decimated when this photograph was taken in February 1987. Hundreds of Routemasters ended up here at Trevor Wigley's yard in 1986/7; writing this caption nearly 17 years later, one is thankful that there are still plenty running in London service today, to witness the type's 50th anniversary. *Geoff Rixon*

Stagecoach joined the Routemaster revival, acquiring five RMs from London Buses to operate local services around Perth. In January 1985 the company purchased a second, much larger batch, comprising 37 RMs (including RM1741 seen here), two RMAs and four one-time Northern General RMF-type buses. At deregulation in October 1986, trading as 'Magicbus', it commenced Routemaster operations in Glasgow with routes 19 and 20 from the city centre to the large housing areas of Easterhouse and Castlemilk; another route was the X70 express from Glasgow to Perth. RM1741 leaves Buchanan bus station on route 19 in April 1987. A year later this bus would be sold to Citilink of Hull, which independent operator was taken over in March 1989 by Kingston-upon-Hull City Transport. Unused by KHCT, RM1741 passed in July 1989 to East Yorkshire Motor Services (809), which in 1994 re-registered it as PAG 809A. Working in passenger service in Hull until August 1995, it was subsequently sold to a dealer who in turn resold it in 1999 to Auto Hobby in Warsaw, Poland, where it remains in use with Target School of English. *Geoff Rixon*

Another Scottish Bus Group subsidiary to take advantage of the availability of Routemasters was Strathtay Scottish, which in 1986 decided to purchase 20 for operation in Perth and Dundee. The stalwarts obviously proved very popular, as in 1987/8 a further 10 were purchased, of which six were for service. One of the first batch, RM1821, is seen in Dundee city centre in April 1987. This bus would never leave Scotland, being scrapped in Dundee by November 1992. *Geoff Rixon*

Three of the one-time BEA fleet — RMAs 11, 37 and 58 — started a new life with independent Verwood Transport, which operator, having converted them for one-person operation, used them on a shopping service in the Bournemouth/Poole area in the summer of 1987. RMA58 is seen in March 1988 working on route 102 *en route* from Poole to Bournemouth. The RMAs would be sold following takeover by Wilts & Dorset in January 1989, but all three would see further service; RMA58, having moved on to Blue Triangle of Bootle in November 1991, would pass to MTL Holdings in May 1994 but since October 1998 has been with Liverpool Motor Services of Aintree. *Geoff Rixon*

In 1988 Burnley & Pendle purchased direct from London Buses six RMs, principally for use on its 23 route, then suffering direct competition from local independents. Painted in a very attractive livery of red and cream, with a theme portraying characters from the popular BBC TV series *EastEnders*, (presumably to emphasise their London origins), they saw just two years' service before being placed in store. RM2114 is seen on the outskirts of Burnley soon after entering service on route 25 in May 1988. This RM is now used by McDonalds in Budapest, Hungary. *Geoff Rixon*

In April 1989 East Yorkshire Motor Services acquired seven Routemasters for Hull routes 56 and 56A, all being purchased direct from London Buses. Given traditional East Yorkshire colours of indigo, primrose and white, six were prepared by Kent Engineering at Canterbury, the seventh receiving similar treatment at London Buses' Edgware garage. RM982, freshly painted in these very attractive colours, is seen in a quiet Hull in its first few days of service on route 56A in May 1988. The fleet would grow to a total of 19 (exclusive of five purchased solely for spares), of which four, painted red and white, were for the Scarborough & District operation. The Hull Routemasters would be replaced in August 1995, and RM982 subsequently exported to Argentina. *Geoff Rixon*

The new London General company was launched in 1989, operating services from Putney, Victoria and Stockwell garages. To celebrate the event two Routemasters — RM89 and RM1590 — received a special pre-1933 livery with large 'GENERAL' fleetnames, operating from Victoria garage on route 11. They made an agreeable sight, especially as by this time there were fewer than 500 standard Routemasters still in London. This lucky picture features them one behind the other in the slip road at Victoria bus station on 6 May 1989. Fitted with an Iveco engine in 1991, RM89 would be sold in July 1994 to old-established Scottish independent McGills of Barrhead. RM1590 later passed to a psychiatric care and support group in Ashford, Middlesex. *Geoff Rixon*

5

The 1990s

ALTHOUGH the 1990s would be significant in terms of the operation of London's bus services, the position with regard to the surviving Routemasters was relatively stable. At the start of the decade, following the success of pilot schemes to update the fleet, most received new engines, and a major refurbishment programme was implemented for all the RMLs to give them an extended life of at least 10 years.

Following tendering in 1993 of routes 19 and 13, London experienced the novelty of Routemasters operating in liveries which were not red (a development subsequently curbed by an edict decreeing that the livery of buses penetrating the Central Zone should be at least 75% — later 80% — red, as the traditional red London bus was at risk of disappearing from the streets). The buses for these routes were renovated RMLs, so it came as a surprise that unrefurbished RMs, whose numbers were still declining (albeit slowly), should be used on route 159

from January 1994. The buses were painted in a red-and-cream livery closely resembling that once carried by the Brighton, Hove & District fleet.

The 11 subsidiaries of London Buses Ltd were privatised between January 1994 and January 1995, and shortly afterwards London Buses Ltd handed over to London Transport Buses its remaining vehicles. These included 30 standard RMs retained as a strategic reserve fleet and 46 RMLs leased to the operators of routes 19 and 13. The RMs were sold in 1997, and some re-entered service in London.

The remainder of the decade saw the continuing withdrawal of provincial Routemasters (only one major operator outside London still using them by 2000) and positive developments in London as a start was made on refurbishing standard RMs.

Yet again, prospects were promising for the London Routemaster as it entered a new decade.

RM6 was first licensed for service in 1959 and 45 years later, in 2004, was still hard at work on the streets of London. For the past decade or so it has worked from Norwood and Brixton garages on routes 137 and 159, operated by South London Transport, which in 1995 was sold to T. Cowie PLC (now Arriva). At the time of the takeover the South London fleet included 31 RMs and 27 RMLs. In January 1985 the decision was taken to paint the RMs in a distinctive livery of red and cream for route 159, displaying the route diagram on advertising panels, and with fluorescent lighting inside. Fitted with an Iveco engine in 1991, RM6 is seen in these colours at Streatham Hill in May 1994; by the end of 1997, when Cowie changed its identity, it had reverted to plain red. Another photograph of this bus appears on page 83. *Geoff Rixon*

In 1993 LT's Tendered Bus Division announced that Kentish Bus had won the contract to operate route 19 (Finsbury Park Station–Battersea Bridge) — the first crew route to be awarded to a private company. To operate the service, which it took over on 24 April, Kentish Bus leased from LT a fleet of 24 RMLs, all fitted with Iveco engines, fully refurbished and painted in its livery of maroon and cream, with a route diagram displayed on the advertising panels. RML2452 is seen on 7 June 1993 in the yard beside the old Battersea garage, used as the 19's southern terminus, which in October was to become the RMLs' base, replacing New Covent Garden Market. In October 1997, with Kentish Bus now part of the Cowie group (later Arriva), the 19 was taken over by fellow subsidiary South London Transport, and by the spring of 1998 the RMLs would revert to red livery, in which they still operate today, supported by a few refurbished RMs. *Geoff Rixon*

In August 1993 it was announced that BTS Coaches of Borehamwood had won the tender to operate route 13 (Aldwych–Golders Green), this being the second Routemaster route to go to a non-London Buses operator. A fleet of 22 RMLs, repainted in a livery of poppy red with yellow relief band and based in a yard at the side of Elstree station, took over operation of the route in December. RML2719, photographed in October 1994, is seen off-route, having been diverted via Marble Arch. In June 1996, following takeover by Yorkshire-based Blazefield Holdings (which already owned parts of the erstwhile London Country Bus Services), BTS was renamed London Sovereign, and in April 1999 its operating base was transferred to the LT-owned garage at Edgware. With re-tendering of the 13 due in early 2000, Sovereign was reluctant to bid to retain it, but with re-tendering postponed to August 2001 it decided to bid and was re-awarded the contract. As part of this agreement the RMLs left route 13, to be replaced by Marshall-refurbished RMs. *Geoff Rixon*

Above left: There is quite a story to tell about RM1183, which with 11 others was sold by London Buses in August/September 1988 to Southend Transport, whose fleet of Routemasters would increase by 1991 to 24, all fitted with Transmatic fluorescent lighting. In 1993 RM1183 was acquired by London & Country for contract work from Leatherhead garage and by 1994 had been repainted in that company's two-tone green, numbered 4109. Used additionally in normal service on routes 406, 414, and 473, following a spell off the road it reappeared in Lincoln green for use on Summer Sunday/Bank Holiday service 465. In 1995 it was sold to Nostalgiabus, which company continued to run it in the same livery. Having sustained roof damage while on rail-replacement work at South Ruislip,

it was repaired in time to work its owner's new Routemaster-operated service 306 (Epsom–Kingston), starting in December 1997. Sadly, however, fate struck again early in 1998, when RM1183 was destroyed by fire in the company's yard at Mitcham. The bus is seen here in happier days, working for London & Country on route 406 in Penrhyn Road, Kingston, in the spring of 1994. *Geoff Rixon*

Above right: Displaying its later London & Country livery of Lincoln green, RM1183 passes along Claremont Road, Surbiton, on an August Bank Holiday Monday 465 journey to Box Hill, Dorking, in 1995. *Geoff Rixon*

The first RM with an Iveco engine to be sold outside London, RM89, by now re-registered as VYJ 893 stands at Renfrew Ferry on 29 June 1995 in service with McGills Bus Services of Barrhead. Used on route 1 (Auchenback–Paisley/Renfrew Ferry), it also promotes Barrhead's centenary. In the late 1990s it would be sold to a buyer in Argentina for use as a promotional vehicle. *Geoff Rixon*

As part of an aid package from the British Government in 1988 the Sri Lanka Transport Board acquired 41 RMs, two of which are shown here in February 1994. By this time most were in very poor condition, not helped by the fact that they were often seriously overloaded. RM2158 typifies this as it pulls away on a peak hour journey in Kandy — a case of 64 seated and 100 standing! — and is believed to be one of the few which remain in service. The second example is a very battered RM333, receiving some attention before leaving Ratmalana depot. *(both) Les Folkard*

In the early 1980s a competitive streak developed between those London bus garages that selected a favoured vehicle — usually a Routemaster — to become their pride and joy as a 'showbus', in the summer months winning awards at rallies all over the country. Some of the top competitors were RM8 (Sidcup), RM83 (Muswell Hill), RM89 (Victoria), RM254 (Kingston and, later, Norbiton), RM737 (Harrow Weald), RM1000 (Croydon) and RM1563 (Mortlake). All are now in preservation, save RM83 and RM89, which now reside in Serbia and Argentina respectively. RM254, owned by your author, has been restored to original 1960s condition and is seen on a photoshoot at Ham Common in 1997. *Geoff Rixon*

In December 1997 Nostalgiabus of Mitcham, which had a fleet of seven Routemasters, mostly for school-contract and rail-replacement work, began a commercial service, route 306, from Epsom to Kingston. Freshly repainted in the company's livery, RM1571 leaves Brook Street, Kingston, in May 1998. Unfortunately this service was short-lived, ending in July 1998, and Nostalgiabus would cease trading altogether in December 2003. Meanwhile RM1571, having been de-roofed in an accident in September 1999, would be rebuilt as an open-topper and is now used for wedding hires. *Geoff Rixon*

Of London Coaches' fleet of 20 open-top RMs used on the Original London Sightseeing Tour, 10 were sent in January 1990 to Canterbury-based Kent Engineering, to be lengthened to provide extra passenger capacity, achieved by adding one standard bay amidships. Thus rebuilt, they were reclassified ERM (the 'E' denoting extended). London Coaches was the first of London Buses' operating subsidiaries to be privatised, being sold to its management in May 1992. In December 1997 its sightseeing operation was sold to Arriva, and since then the Routemaster fleet has dwindled, being replaced by Metrobuses. Arriva livery was nevertheless applied to Routemasters from Easter 1999, ERM237 being seen thus, branded for the Original London Sightseeing Tour, at Marble Arch in June 1999. Having left London in 2002, many of the Routemaster fleet, including all the ERMs, are now at work with Lothian Buses' Mac Tours operation in Edinburgh. *Geoff Rixon*

The Big Bus Company, based at Earlsfield in South West London, operates its own London sightseeing tours, for which it maintains a large fleet of pristine vehicles, including some ex-Northern General Routemasters. Among these is Leyland-engined FPT 588C (now numbered RMF588), which left Northern General as long ago as July 1978. Sold to dealer Ensign of Grays, it was resold to Brakell of Cheam, which dealer numbered it RMF2794 and hired it to LT for use on the Round London Sightseeing Tour. By 1981 it had spent two years with Prince Marshall's Obsolete Fleet, also on London sightseeing work; then, in October 1983, it was sold to Omnibus Promotions (dealer) and by January 1985 had been resold to a Christian Fellowship group at Tower Hamlets. In January 1987 it was purchased (again for London sightseeing work) by Blue Triangle of Rainham (Essex), which converted it to an open-top before selling it to Big Bus in April 1992. It is seen emerging from Park Lane at Marble Arch in August 1999. *Geoff Rixon*

The Big Bus Company's second Routemaster purchase, in February 1995, was 'RMF592' (FPT 592C), which had been in preservation since 1981 and had been fitted with an AEC engine to replace its Leyland original. This bus, like the third example — 'RMF603' (FPT 603C), acquired from preservationists in December 1996 — has retained its roof, being used mostly for winter sightseeing work, and is seen at Hyde Park Corner. *Geoff Rixon*

6

The 2000s

THE new millennium opened on a sad note for Routemasters: Reading Mainline, by now owned by Reading Buses, ceased using RMs on 22 July 2000. Having commenced operations on 23 July 1994, the company's fleet of Routemasters numbered 43 at its height. Ironically some returned to London.

Yet another major organisational change for London's buses occurred on 3 July 2000. A local administration for London was re-introduced, and its leader, the Mayor of London, was the former leader of the abolished GLC, Ken Livingstone. The Mayor assumed responsibility for London Bus Services Ltd and a new organisation called Transport for London (TfL). It soon became apparent that Mr Livingstone, recognising the benefits of crew operation, was a Routemaster supporter, and longer-term proposals, following an acknowledgement that the RM could not last forever, included the development of a 'Son of Routemaster' or, to be politically correct, 'Child of Routemaster'!

On 22 September 2000 came the news, from TfL, that all Routemaster enthusiasts wanted to hear: the Routemaster was safe, with the prospect of its operation until 2010. TfL officials wasted no time in providing evidence of this commitment, abandoning the planned introduction of low-floor buses on route 7 and scouring the country for redundant or preserved RMs for reacquisition. These were to be completely refurbished and put back in service in response to the planned expansion of Central London routes. In February 2001, by which time 33 RMs had been bought back, Marshall of Cambridge was awarded the contract to renovate and upgrade these vehicles. The work included the fitting of new engines and gearboxes, as well as modern lighting and new windows. The first 21 were introduced on route 13, replacing RMLs which were then redistributed among various London operators.

A return to a special livery, after an absence of many years, occurred in 2002 when 50 London buses were outshopped in gold to commemorate HM The Queen's Golden Jubilee. The total included 15 Routemasters, of which 13 were RMLs, but all bar RM6 were covered in gold vinyl rather than actually painted gold.

In September 1994 London Buses' East London company was acquired by Stagecoach. Included in its fleet were three of the seven RMCs that had been used on 'Beckton Express' route X15, operated from March 1989 to November 1991. Following the Stagecoach takeover all three — RMC1456/61/85 — operated for almost a decade alongside RMs and RMLs on busy trunk route 15, until Routemaster operation ceased at the end of August 2003. RMC1456 (re-registered in 1994 as LFF 875) is seen Paddington-bound in the Strand in August 2000; heading in the opposite direction is RML2555 of First CentreWest on the 23, which would lose its Routemasters on 14 November 2003. RMC1456 has now found a new home in preservation in Surrey. *Geoff Rixon*

Metroline Travel was purchased from LT by a management-led team in October 1994. Following various takeovers, most notably of neighbouring ex-London Buses company London Northern, Metroline Holdings was itself taken over in February 2000 by Singapore-based transport group DelGro. The company acquired a Routemaster fleet comprising 71 RMLs and nine RMs, operated on routes 6, 10 and 98 from Willesden and Holloway garages. In Metroline's distinctive livery with blue skirt and front grille mesh, RML2419 is seen fresh from repaint on route 10 at Hyde Park Corner in August 2000. The 10 would lose its Routemasters in January 2003. *Geoff Rixon*

Bad news for Routemaster lovers arrived on 30 September 2002, when the Mayor of London announced that RMs were due to be replaced on all routes, except for one or two tourist routes. This represented a complete reversal of the policy announced two years earlier and clearly reflected new attitudes to OPO working on Central London routes arising from off-bus ticketing, reduced traffic levels (following the introduction of Congestion Charging) and the need for expensive mechanical renewal of Routemaster engines and transmissions. Subsequent announcements (in October 2002) clarified the position somewhat, drawing attention both to the proposed introduction of 'smartcards' (which would render conductors superfluous) and to opposition to RMs from organisations representing the disabled.

However, TfL did not envisage articulated buses completely replacing the iconic Routemaster and suggested that some way of retaining some of these vehicles would be found.

The new policy finally came into effect in August 2003, when the Routemasters on route 15 — a favourite with enthusiasts due to the use of a Green Line-liveried RMC — were replaced by low-floor OPO buses. Later in the year routes 11 and 23 lost their RMLs and, ironically, in the Routemaster's 50th-anniversary year, most of the remaining Routemaster-operated routes will see these vehicles replaced. However, a few central routes should manage to retain their Routemasters until 2005, and it is hoped that some heritage routes will be introduced to enable the Routemaster to maintain at least a limited presence on London's streets.

Reading Mainline commenced operations in and around Reading on 23 July 1994. The company eventually amassed a fleet of 43 Routemasters, from various sources — Southend Transport, Strathtay Scottish, Blackpool Transport, London Buses (via Barnsley dealer PVS) and even preservationists. The operation was sold to Reading Buses in June 1998, but Routemaster-operated services continued for a further two years. The final day of operation was Saturday 22 July 2000, when 11 vehicles, complete with wreaths on their radiator grilles, were operational; RM244, photographed turning into Craven Road near the terminus of route D, is now preserved in Bridgend, Wales. *Geoff Rixon*

RM1919 was overhauled and converted to open-top for the London Coaches sightseeing fleet in 1986. By 2000 it was operated by Arriva from Wandsworth garage on behalf of Harrods, which store had spared no expense in refurbishing it — with tables and new leather-upholstered seats with headrests — for use on its own sightseeing service. The bus is seen in Upper Thames Street in August 2000.
Geoff Rixon

Despite the refurbishment costs, RM1919 remained in operation for just one season, after which it was sold on to Kilby's Executive Travel, based at Hurn Airport, Bournemouth, where, repainted in a very smart silver livery and named the 'Silver Lady', it was photographed in 2002.
In 2003 it would be sold again, passing to a buyer in Austria.
Geoff Rixon

RM120, sold by London Buses in August 1985, was acquired by an advertising company based in Maidstone, Kent, which had it converted to open-top. In January 1988 it was acquired by the London Bus Preservation Group at Cobham, which used it for private hire. In 1994 it was repainted white, branded for LilyWhites and LBM, to operate a service in connection with the All-England Lawn Tennis Championships at Wimbledon. In 1996 it passed to Capital Citybus, which company re-registered it as SSL 809. In 2001, while allocated to Northumberland Park depot, the RM found itself in service working a few journeys on route 91 and also, for one day only — 25 June — route 76, being seen here on Waterloo Bridge. *Geoff Rixon*

Over the years every colour imaginable must have been applied to the Routemaster, but by 2001 it seemed unlikely that there could be any further variations in London, given the '80%-red' rule by then in force. However, in March RML2716 appeared in all-over black to promote the work of human-rights organisation Amnesty International, operating from Clapton garage on route 38 (Clapton–Victoria), which passes AI's offices in Islington. The bus is seen turning into Buckingham Palace Road in May 2001. *Geoff Rixon*

In one of the most surprising developments in the long history of the Routemaster, Transport for London, wishing to increase frequencies on crew-operated services yet faced with a shortfall of Routemasters, decided in 2000 to buy back RMs from wherever they could be found, scouring the country for suitable vehicles and even approaching private owners at bus rallies! Indeed, several preserved examples were purchased, along with redundant vehicles from other operators and dealers. With no central works, they headed to Marshall of Cambridge for complete refurbishment, being fitted with new Cummins B-series Euro 2 engines and Allison automatic gearboxes; the interiors were also completely revamped. Some 21 were for route 13, operated by London Sovereign, based at the TfL-owned garage at Edgware, RM23 being seen entering the Strand in August 2001. This vehicle, which had worked in the Kingston area since overhauled in the 1980s, was withdrawn as a training bus in November 1994 and was re-registered as JFO 256 upon sale in 1995 to Reading Mainline, which operated the bus until its return to London in October 2000.
Geoff Rixon

RM1357, which worked out of Victoria (GM) garage prior to withdrawal in April 1987, was sold in March 1988 to Blackpool Transport, for which it worked until stored in 1994; in 1996 it was purchased by the up-and-coming Reading Mainline, which it served until the end on 22 July 2000. It was then sold to a group of Sea Scouts, the interior being converted to resemble that of a submarine; the effect is so realistic that it is difficult to believe that one is still inside a Routemaster! Used for training purposes, it is seen visiting Cobham Bus Museum for the Routemaster Operators & Owners Association event in July 2001.
Geoff Rixon

Timebus Travel of Watford owns three Routemasters — RM479 (WSJ 737), RM1871 (ALD 871B) and RMA37 (KGJ 612D) — used for private-hire and contract work. All three are maintained to a very high standard, as apparent from this view of RM479, the latest acquisition. A former London Coaches convertible open-topper, it was purchased in May 1999 and was photographed in St Albans in August 2001.
Vernon Murphy

With the advent of HM The Queen's Golden Jubilee in 2002 there was speculation as to whether any of London's buses would celebrate the occasion. Transport for London was duly approached by the Golden Jubilee office about the possibility of having some gold buses, on a similar basis to the silver RMs which had celebrated HM's Silver Jubilee in 1977. The 50 buses selected were mostly OPO types but included 12 RMLs and three RMs, sponsored by four different advertisers plus Transport for London itself. The only downside to all this was that the gold was achieved by the application of vinyl sheeting instead of paint; not only did the colour look flat, but without proper preparation the buses' numerous dents and gashes showed through. RM6, however, was selected for special treatment: for the Jubilee parade on 4 June (wherein it was joined by five other gold buses) it had the gold vinyl removed and was *hand*-painted, and what a difference this made! Looking resplendent in its freshly applied gold livery, it is seen later in the month in Oxford Street, displaying TfL's own advertising, while based at Brixton garage for routes 137 and 159. In June 2003 RM6 would be repainted, again in gold but this time with a mauve relief band. *Dave Brown*

RML2431 was one of the 12 RMLs covered in gold vinyl for Jubilee year. Sponsored by Marks & Spencer and based at Willesden garage for routes 6 and 98, it is seen passing Marble Arch on 19 June 2002. *Geoff Rixon*

Sri Lanka aside, Canada has been the most popular destination for exported Routemasters, being home to 39 RMs and two RCLs residing with various tour operators. The largest number went to Double Deck Tours at Niagara Falls, which had 16 RMs and two RCLs, kept in superb condition. This photograph, taken at the company's depot in August 2000, shows a line-up of four, displaying London blinds and looking absolutely pristine. From right to left are RMs 1909, 1102, 1651 and 1681. Observant readers may spot that RM1651 has received a replacement roof (from an RTW!), following accident damage. *Vernon Murphy*

This extremely smart Routemaster, RM1620, is owned by Abegweit Sightseeing Tours of Charlotte Town, Prince Edward Island, Canada, which company owns two of the country's 41 Routemasters. Working alongside a fleet of RTs and RTLs, RM1620 and its companion (RM1371) were exported in 1983. *Vernon Murphy*

The USA has 24 standard RMs spread across the country and in its territories. Even the first production body (of RM5), which operated last in London from Brixton as RM47 in 1992, now serves snacks in the US Virgin Islands. Iveco-engined RM591, fitted with a sliding central door on the (UK) offside, is seen working for Daisy Tours in San Antonio, Texas, in September 2002. *Trevor Muir*

Some 15 Routemasters have found themselves in Argentina, used mainly for tourist work, these being among the more recent exports. RM1266 is seen in San Martin de Los Andes on a Redbus city tour on 26 February 2002. *Anna Pawlyn*

New Zealand has just three Routemasters. RM221 arrived there in 1993 and survives as a hamburger bar at Wanaka Airfield, while RM1670 was exported nearly 20 years ago and is available for hire as a party bus. The third, RM1660, has been in New Zealand for 18 years and is used as a tour and post bus; looking very smart after a repaint in November 2000, it is pictured on sightseeing work between Queenstown and Arrowtown at Lake Hayes, with the appropriately named Remarkables mountain range as a backdrop. *Vernon Murphy*

Iveco-engined RM1101 was sold by London Buses in September 1994, last working from Upton Park garage. Acquired by A1A Travel of Birkenhead for use on school-contract work, it was re-registered for the second time in 1995 (from KGH 969A to KFF 367), having surrendered its original mark while still in London. By June 1997 it had been acquired by friends of the Wirral Transport Museum, who, having restored it to LT red with cream relief band, used it on Sundays and Bank Holiday Mondays on a service (15) between Woodside Ferry and New Brighton. In June 2002 it received Golden Jubilee livery, as seen here at that year's Showbus rally at Duxford. *Geoff Rixon*

Below left: The market square in Poznan, Poland, is one of the last places one would expect to find a Routemaster but in 2002 was host to none other than RM1983, once the flagship of LT's 50th-anniversary celebrations. In fact Poland is home to a number of Routemasters (15 RMs and one RMC), six of which were imported by an advertising agency in August 1999, while Norwich Union had a contract to promote pensions. RM1983 can be seen in its earlier glory on page 65. *Alan Davies*

Below right: RM102 was sold as early as September 1985 to DPR International of Bromley for use as a hospitality vehicle. Converted to open-top, it still carries its original registration, even though it now resides in France, having since 2000 worked for Bateaux-Mouches, an operator of Parisian river cruises. It is pictured by the Seine in September 2003, with the Eiffel Tower as a backdrop. *Jo Rixon*

A sight which sadly could not be repeated for the Routemaster's 50th anniversary in 2004. Taken from high up in the offices in Eastbourne Terrace, Paddington, in September 2001, the photograph depicts two Stagecoach vehicles — RM1527 and an unidentified RML — on route 15, which would lose its Routemasters on 31 August 2003. Also visible are two CentreWest RMLs on route 23, upon which Routemaster operation would cease with effect from 14 November 2003.
Vernon Murphy

Early in 2002 Edinburgh sightseeing company Mac Tours, then based at Cockenzie (but now part of Lothian Buses), purchased all 10 of the Arriva (formerly London Coaches) ERM open-toppers, along with five open-top standard RMs and closed-top RCL2248 — a fleet of 16 at this stage. The erstwhile ERM281 (now Mac Tours 10) is seen freshly into service in George Street in September 2002. Late in 2003 a start would be made on fitting the ERMs with Cummins B-series engines. *Dave Brown*

Mac Tours' new Britannia Tour service began in December 2002, using Routemasters fitted with platform doors and painted in a smart livery of blue and yellow with red wheels. To date (July 2004) this livery is carried by ERM94, RMC1485 (acquired in August 2003 from Stagecoach in London), two RMAs (9 and 50) and four RMs (371, 727, 1010 and 2210), RM2210 being seen unloading passengers at Ocean Terminal in June 2003. Sold to Clydeside Scottish in October 1987, this bus passed in June 1992 to East Yorkshire, which operator converted it to open-top for its seafront service in Scarborough; at the end of the 2001 summer season it was sold to Barnsley-based dealer PVS, from which Mac Tours purchased it in 2002. *Dave Brown*

In June 2002 Mac Tours purchased from Stagecoach Bluebird one-time BEA Routemaster NMY 634E, which since October 1994 had been part of the Stagecoach preserved fleet and based at the Scottish Bus Museum at Lathalmond. It now works (as Mac Tours 20) on the Britannia Tour service and was photographed at Leith Docks, just after being painted in its new livery in September 2002. *Vernon Murphy*

Another photograph of a Mac Tours Routemaster on the Britannia Tour, taken in Edinburgh's Princes Street in September 2003. Showing its newly fitted platform doors, 803 DYE is not all it seems, as the real RM1803 is no more, having being scrapped in 1992; however, Mac Tours wanted an original LT registration for RM1010, which had lost its own original mark while with Kelvin Scottish in 1987. A similar situation applies to Mac Tours' RM727, now registered 858 DYE, which properly belongs to RM1858, scrapped in August 1994. *Dave Brown*

RM1069, withdrawn from London Buses' New Cross garage in December 1986 and sold for preservation in February 1987, was purchased in 1995 by Dean Sullivan, who in 1999 set up Sullivan Buses from a base at South Mimms in Hertfordshire. The Routemaster is used mainly for private-hire and rail-replacement work but in October 2002 was captured on a rare outing on stage-carriage work, being seen near the Abbots Langley terminus of route W4 from Watford. The company also owns an ex-Stagecoach Routemaster, RML2272, which it bought in May 2003 after it was withdrawn due to accident damage, this being the first RML sold from London in the 21st century. The vehicle was fully rebuilt and repainted and worked, for one day only (20 December 2003), on Armchair's Chessington–Kingston Christmas Park & Ride service (K50). *Hayden Davis*

Until recently Stagecoach East London had a fleet of 54 RMLs, five RMs and three RMCs for crew routes 8 and 15, operated from Bow and Upton Park garages. RMC1461, which had been repainted in its original Green Line livery in 1994, continued working on route 15 for nine years, until the Routemasters gave way to new low-floor vehicles at the end of August 2003, when it was retired from service and donated to Cobham Bus Museum. This unusual view, recorded from an office block in Eastbourne Terrace, Paddington, shows it approaching the terminus of route 15 in May 2003. *Vernon Murphy*

In late 2002 TfL was still on the lookout for more Routemasters, in order to meet increased peak vehicle requirements on certain routes, and managed to obtain a further half dozen RMs — RM54 and RM1975 from preservationists, RM346 and RM713, which had returned to the UK from Italy, RM85 from Blue Triangle and RM1292 from Mediabus of Croydon. With the demise of Marshall, the Cambridge-based company which had refurbished the previous 40 or so RMs, these six had mechanical and bodywork refurbishment carried out at Arriva's Norwood and Enfield garages, with Cummins itself fitting new B-series engines. Three — RM1292, RM1975 and RM54 — entered service during 2003, working from Battersea garage on route 19, the others eventually following suit in March 2004.

Top left: Seen here in preservation is RM54, in traditional Blackburn Corporation colours! Although this (or any other) Routemaster never worked for Blackburn, its owner did and decided to apply this very attractive livery to his RM. This photograph was taken at the Wallace Arnold premises (now closed) in Geldard Road, Leeds, this being the starting-point for the 1994 Leeds–Huddersfield rally. *Malcolm King*

Lower left: Following refurbishment RM54 would return to the streets of London in 2003, being seen in Sloane Street on route 19 in July that year. *Geoff Rixon*

Another surprise was in store from Stagecoach London in August 2003. Just as its green-liveried RMC had finished service on route 15, RML2456, which had started life in 1966 in the Country Area, found itself back in Lincoln green (and this at a time when every bus employed on TfL contracts has to be 80%-red!). Looking resplendent, it was photographed outside the RAF Club in Piccadilly in September 2003, by which time it had been at work for two weeks on Stagecoach's surviving Routemaster route (8) from Bow garage. Regrettably the 8 would also lose its Routemasters, in June 2004. *Vernon Murphy*

Nowadays restricted to appearances at special events, in March 2004 London Central's RM9 was called upon to help out on Red Arrow route 507; this was necessitated by the temporary withdrawal (for modification) of the company's articulated Mercedes-Benz Citaros, after three of the latter had burst into flames while in service. This view was recorded in Bressenden Place, Victoria. *Vernon Murphy*

In April 2004, to mark 50 years of the Routemaster, First London RM1650 took a step back in time, being repainted in 1977 Silver Jubilee livery as SRM3 as part of a joint venture with BAA to promote the Paddington–Heathrow Express rail service. The bus is seen on 15 May in Acton on First London's (by then) sole surviving Routemaster route, the 7, which was due to be converted to low-floor operation from 3 July. *Geoff Rixon*

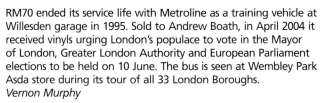

RM70 ended its service life with Metroline as a training vehicle at Willesden garage in 1995. Sold to Andrew Boath, in April 2004 it received vinyls urging London's populace to vote in the Mayor of London, Greater London Authority and European Parliament elections to be held on 10 June. The bus is seen at Wembley Park Asda store during its tour of all 33 London Boroughs. *Vernon Murphy*

Last used by London Transport in 1984, RCL2223 has since had no fewer than eight different owners, the latest of which is the Heathrow Airport Ltd. Used as an information vehicle in connection with the new Terminal 5 building under construction at Heathrow, the bus was photographed — complete with 'Airport Routemaster' fleetnames — on the A4 at Slough in May 2004. *Vernon Murphy*

Displaced from route 23 by low-floor buses with effect from 14 November 2003, eight of First London's RMLs moved north to join First Glasgow, for use on private-hire work from the latter's Kingswood depot. However, in May 2004 one of these — RML2365 — was painted in full Glasgow Corporation livery for use on the Glasgow city tour, being seen so employed in North Hanover Street on the 15th of that month.
Alan Millar

On Friday 4 June 2004 Stagecoach in London's surviving Routemasters finished work on route 8 (thereafter operated by low-floor vehicles) and were given quite a send-off. Making a surprise appearance alongside some 20 historic London buses was RML2665, freshly attired in private-hire livery and seen here arriving at Victoria. This bus has since received standard Stagecoach 'national' livery, although at the time of writing (July 2004) its future use was uncertain.
Geoff Rixon

Having spent the preceding 10 years working from Brixton garage on routes 137 and 159, Arriva's RM275 was withdrawn from service in May 2004, whereupon it was cleverly disguised as a triple-decker to promote the film *Harry Potter and the Prisoner of Azkaban*, attending the film's première at Leicester Square on 30 May. The bus is seen at North Weald on 27 June. *Geoff Rixon*

In July 2004 RM3 emerged from overhaul restored to original condition as RML3, complete with 1956-style front end. This represented the culmination of a project instigated two years earlier by Andy Baxter of the Cobham Bus Museum, which owns the vehicle. Displaying blinds for route 8, on which it originally worked, the bus is seen in all its glory at the RM50 rally at Finsbury Park on 24 July. *Geoff Rixon*

Considerable surprise was caused by the appearance, in time for the RM50 rally, of two of Arriva's Routemasters in special liveries for use on route 19, which terminates at Finsbury Park.

Right: Having been withdrawn earlier in July, RM25 re-emerged (registered as UXC 855) in an unusual livery of chocolate brown, cream, yellow and black recalling the Great Northern Railway's horse buses of the 1850s, which ran between King's Cross and London Bridge. The RM is seen in Rock Street, Finsbury Park, on 25 July. *Geoff Rixon*

Right: The other Arriva Routemaster to appear in a special livery was RML2524. This celebrates the 175th anniversary of George Shillibeer's original horse-drawn 'Omnibus' service but has been treated to a contemporary rendition which differs from the scheme applied to RMs in 1979. The bus is seen leaving Finsbury Park bus station on Saturday 24 July, its first day in service. *Geoff Rixon*

Below: A long line of Routemasters at Finsbury Park on the occasion of the 'RM50 Spectacular' rally, held by the Routemaster Operators & Owners Association on 24/25 July 2004. Nearest the camera are RML2760, the last Routemaster built, RM470, which had travelled specially from Germany, and RM7, making its first public appearance since sale for preservation in 1985. Although, with the run-down of London's Routemaster fleet, 2004 has provoked bitter-sweet emotions, the event provided a fitting tribute to the type in its Golden Jubilee year. *Geoff Rixon*